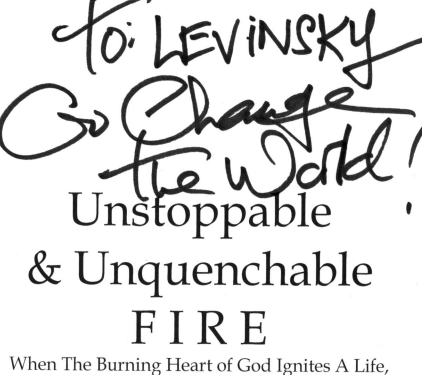

To: LEVINSKY

Go Change the World!

Unstoppable
& Unquenchable
FIRE

When The Burning Heart of God Ignites A Life,
Invades our Cities & Recaptures A Nation.

Heb
12:28-29

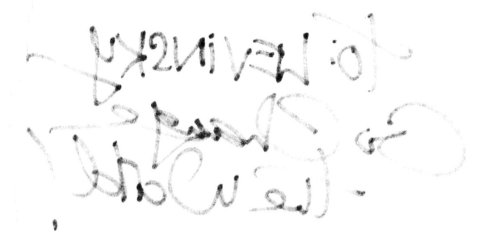

Published by Brian & Bren Gibbs
Light The Fire Ministries
P.O. Box 51586 | Sarasota, FL 34232

www.lightthefireministries.org
IGNITING Revival | EQUIPPING Leaders | RESCUING The Broken

Dedication
To The Burning Hearts

I dedicate this book to the new breed of emerging pioneers, revivalists and firebrands that are braving and overcoming every adversity to bring the Gospel of the Kingdom to the Nations! May you never lose hope! May you never give up, and may you keep the fire burning! May the grace and fire of the Lord make you an instrument of blessing and transformation to our generation and generations yet to come! The Kingdom of God was always meant to shape culture, never to retreat from it. Forward!

"*Unstoppable & Unquenchable Fire is the testimony of a life written on pages to be shared with others, so they too can encounter the All Consuming One. It is the story of Brian Gibbs' life, which I have seen first hand since the time we met over 22 years ago. This book is not merely ideas and thoughts to ponder; it is real, tangible and the essence of who Brian is and what God has embedded on the inside of him. I have seen Brian be ignited by the fire, pursue the fire, stir the fire, protect the fire, and give it away, so others can encounter their Loving, Heavenly Father. That is the purpose of this book – for you to be ignited by the fire of His Love, commit to keep the fire burning, be stirred with the purpose of the fire on your life, and be taught to protect the fire at all costs, so it can change the world around you. Brian's life, journey, encounters, and testimonies of Jesus has changed my life, and I believe it will change your life too!*"

Bren Gibbs
Wife & Co-founder | Light The Fire Ministries

"*This book begins by sharing Brian Gibbs' family's testimony and his personal experience of his hunger for God. His quest for God has exposed his heart to a perspective of heaven that carries hope, revival, and preparation for another great awakening for America. Brian shares radical testimonies of miracles and places readers in a position of responsibility to stand in their role and function to bring the kingdom of heaven to earth. This family wonderfully illustrates what it is to love God with everything you have and are, becoming a prototype for this next generation.*"

Bill Johnson
Bethel Church
Author, When Heaven Invades Earth
Redding, CA

"*Brian Gibbs is a revivalist in every sense of the word! We have known Brian for many years and his heart relentlessly burns to see the heavens open and the next Great Awakening come to the earth! This book, "Unstoppable and Unquenchable Fire", will stir up a fresh hunger within to you to pursue the heart of God along side of Brian! As David Crowder's song, "Roaring Like A Lion" says, Brian's book thunders the anthem and prophetic call - "Let Heaven roar and fire fall, come shake the ground with the sound of Revival!*"

David & Kathie Thomas
Victory Christian Center
Bishop & Lead Pastors
Youngstown, OH

"As we see in Hebrews 1:7, the Lord causes his servants to be like fiery flames. Brian Gibbs is certainly part of this company; a cadre on the earth today burning bright with Heaven's passion. His book expresses the cry of a ravished heart unwilling to live without the consuming fire of first love. As you read Unstoppable & Unquenchable Fire, each page will challenge and encourage you to leave behind all comfort zones and status quo mindsets! Brian's words are like burning torches lighting the way for this generation, and summoning them into a great reformation.

Let this book teach and inspire you into new depths of passion, hope and holy wonder as you trust Jesus for everything that He paid for. This is a call for that which is required to transform our culture and ultimately heal cities and nations in biblical proportions. You will not regret answering this Heavenly invitation!"

Georgian Banov
President and Co-Founder of Global Celebration
General Director of The Bulgarian Bible Project
Harrisburg, PA

"In his debut book "Unstoppable & Unquenchable Fire" Brian Gibbs retraces for us his personal, passionate and palpable journey into the fire of God's presence. Some men make truth sterile theory which is about as satisfying as offering a hungry man a toothpick. Brian on the other hand incites hunger for God's presence as he retraces his times of wandering and even wondering. The title of the book captures the essence of Brian Gibbs, truly a burning one. I have had the privilege of collaborating with some of the premier voices of revival in the last few years and consider Brian to be a leader of the emerging generation of revivalists. He is one among a few worthy to take the baton. By the time you finish the last page of the last chapter I suspect you too will be ignited!"

Dr. Randall Worley
Randall Worley Ministries
Fort Mill, SC

"When I finished the manuscript for "Unstoppable & Unquenchable Fire," I felt the wind of the Spirit blowing over the embers of my spirit. I have known Brian Gibbs for a lot of years, and the way I met him was through revival. I have often said, "Once you have had your feet under the table of revival, no other table will ever satisfy." It is clear that Brian has had his feet under that table! His pen is like a match that lights fires in every chapter! I am encouraged to know that Brian is in possession of sparks that will help ignite revival, and even an awakening to his generation!"

John A. Kilpatrick
John Kilpatrick Ministries
Daphne, AL

"I have known Brian for many years now, or at least I thought I did. I've known him as a loving passionate pastor and a flaming revivalist. What I didn't know was the backstory…how young he was when the flame was lit and what has fueled his lifetime of passion. From the opening story of his childhood to the last challenge of the last chapter this book details the journey of a true "God Chaser". I know one when I see one. May the furious flame from His heart ignite your heart!"

Tommy Tenney
God Chasers Network
Pineville, LA

"Read this book and you will never settle for normal again! Holy fire will stand next to you refusing to give access to the god of false contentment. Brian Gibbs is my dear friend and a man consumed with Holy passion to see the body of Christ healed and made whole."

Ivan Tait
What Matters Missions & Ministries
Colorado Springs, CO

"In Unstoppable & Unquenchable Fire, Brian Gibbs will take you to a place of hunger for a fresh move of God — starting in your own heart. He will make you long for revival, and inspire a desire to lay yourself on the altar with a promise to go anywhere and do anything God desires. This book is a great reminder that just one touch from Him is not enough. We need more. Brian's present ministry is bearing the fruit of his encounters with the Holy Spirit. In the pages of this book, he reveals the God who loves you and that "His love is an unstoppable, unquenchable fire!" Reading this book created hunger in my own heart for another encounter with the Holy Spirit!"

Dr. Tom Jones
Executive Director, Global Awakening
Harrisburg, PA

"Occasionally you meet someone whose passion for Jesus infects and energizes every heart. Such is the case with Brian Gibbs. His writings arrive from years of pastoral experience and as a seasoned revivalist, but his impartation is fresh and invigorating. The principles in this book are the substance of Brian's life and the intention of the gospel. When Brian writes, you feel the certainty of someone with intimate knowledge of God's ways. Unstoppable & Unquenchable Fire is a gift to those who wonder about the future of the church or anyone who needs faith strengthened. As you read Unstoppable & Unquenchable Fire, expect fresh experiences with the Presence of the Holy One."

Pastor Jim Hennesy
Trinity Church
Cedar Hill, TX

"To say that Brian Gibbs is a passionate preacher of the Gospel is like saying a nuclear bomb makes a loud noise. Intertwined with humor and wisdom, this is the story that lit the fire, and as a fellow child of the 80's, it was a pleasure to read. I deeply respect Brian's vulnerability and character, and while he has lived enough life to be a father to many, he stands on the edge of becoming one of the most vital and powerful emerging voices of this generation."

William Vanderbush
William Vanderbush Ministries
Austin, TX

"Unstoppable & Unquenchable Fire is a testament of what God can do when just one person turns his heart towards God & His Word - it can change the course and destiny of his own life, the lives of his family and the world! God is searching for men and women who will turn their hearts fully towards Him!"

Karen Gibbs
Mother of Brian Gibbs
Pekin, IL

"*After reading my son's book it set my heart ablaze again, leaving me with wanting more of the fire of God in my own life. This book is a testimony of what God can do in a believer's life if he or she is willing and obedient to follow God. Dare to step out of the dead religious church and be used by God with signs and wonders, and miracle working power to set the captives free. God is looking for people that are full of the Holy Ghost and fire that will demonstrate His love and grace to a lost and dying world that so desperately needs Him.*"

David Gibbs
Father of Brian Gibbs
Pekin, IL

Author's Note

Some of the names of people mentioned in this book have been changed. I've done so where I felt anonymity is essential.

To the international reader: Many of the present day issues that are addressed here in this book are directly correlated to America, but they can be universally applied. God longs for awakening and reformation, in every nation of the world.

Deep Honor & Love to God's friend & messenger
Rev. Miles Black
July 3, 1946 – August 9, 2014
I love you!

Table of Contents

Endorsements

Foreword
By Dutch Sheets
Introduction

Foreword

By Dutch Sheets

There is most certainly a third Great Awakening coming to America and other nations of the world. Like the prophet Elijah, those who have ears to hear the sound of the Holy Spirit above the clamor of the world, know that we have already entered the initial stage. Before there was even a cloud in the sky, Elijah said, *"there is a sound of abundance of rain,"* (1 Kings 18:41). You must hear the sound before you become the voice.

When reading *Unstoppable & Unquenchable Fire*, it becomes abundantly clear that Brian truly is an "Elijah voice" God has raised up to sound a clarion call to a generation thirsty for rain. Many believers today are wearied by the shallow and anemic version of 21st century American Christianity that has produced such a spiritual drought in our land. Unbelievers are not the problem in America; the savorless salt and dim light of the church has been our problem. Brian does a great job of exposing this false expression of the gospel, but he does more than simply "curse the darkness," as the old proverb warns us against. He also does more than the proverb's solution, "light a candle." Brian Gibbs has built a bonfire! Like Elijah, he has rebuilt the ancient altar of the Lord, which has been torn down (see 1 Kings 18:30), and has dared to cry out for fire from heaven (verse 37)!

Like many, I have been guilty at times of simply venting my anger and frustration over our apostate state of affairs in America. I suppose to a degree this is to be expected. But we also need voices of hope that point the way back to the ancient path of truth. Yes, Elijahs can be ruthless with the truth – and Brian has certainly wielded that sword of the Spirit – but they also chart a course for change and remind us of the supernatural, miracle-working power of God available to bring the change. Then taking hope to a higher level, they *offer the promise of fresh rain if we respond.* True prophetic voices are agents of hope.

Beginning with Brian's and his parents' extraordinary conversions

– which in and of themselves are worth the price of this book – you will find yourself inspired and encouraged to believe in the goodness and grace of God. Laced with many other testimonies of God's miraculous power, this book will have you believing God absolutely can save your family, friends, and yes, a nation!

Apart from the above great qualities, however, what gives me even more excitement about this book is the hope it contains for reformation. *Awakening* is the renewal of the church and the salvation of the world; *reformation* is the transformation of society and shaping of culture...the discipling of nations. Jesus said in Matthew 28:18-20: And Jesus came up and spoke to them, saying, *"All authority has been given to Me in heaven and on earth. Go therefore and make disciples of all the nations, baptizing them in the name of the Father and the Son and the Holy Spirit, teaching them to observe all that I commanded you; and lo, I am with you always, even to the end of the age."*

In the last great outpouring of the Holy Spirit – the Jesus People and Charismatic movements – we experienced awakening. Because we had no understanding of transforming a nation, however, we never progressed to reformation. Therefore, while we were seeing our nation *awakened,* the world around us was busy *reforming* it. Awakening changes the heart, reformation shapes the mind. While we sought conversions, the secularists, humanists and liberals reformed government, education, media, the family and much more. The result? Ultimately, we lost a generation. Brian makes clear in the book this need of marrying awakening and reformation.

Lastly, he explains well the need for, and role of, spiritual fathers and mothers. Like Elijah, they will raise up, train and empower the Elisha's and Jehu's of our day – mature sons and daughters that will do more than those of us who preceded them. This power-ful teaching is so very timely! The fact that fresh voices, like Brian, are sounding this clear note gives me amazing hope for true and lasting change.

Read this book! Let the truth it contains awaken and fan the flame of the Holy Spirit in you. Allow the passion Brian releases to prepare your heart for the great awakening that is here – and coming.

For Awakening & Reformation,
Dutch Sheets

Introduction

God's all consuming Love is unstoppable and unquenchable! To be enveloped by His burning love is our destiny. It is a Love that is not of this world. He is pure, immaculate, perfect, undefiled, matchless and holy. God's love for us is immeasurable and unfathomable to such a degree that it transcends human understanding. His dream is that we will fall into His embrace and pleasures and to cleave unto Him with all our heart and strength.

For many years, I have studied revival history and phenomena and the remarkable testimonies that have given witness of heavenly invasions in the earth. Many of my friends are leaders and pioneers in renewal and revival movements around the world. I have mountains of books in my office that are highlighted, underlined and stained with tears, as the Holy Spirit courted my heart and ignited burning hunger in my own personal quest for hosting His Presence. There are so many rich and wonderful books that fill my office written of the great pioneers, revival phenomena and adventures of the likes of Count Zinzendorf, John Huss, Hernhutt & The Moravians, John & Charles Wesley, William Seymour, Frank Bartlemen, Azusa Street, Evan Roberts & The Welsh Revival, John Alexander Dowie, George Jeffreys, Charles

Finney, Captain Jack Sparrow & Bilbo Baggins…haha, I wanted to make sure you are reading with focus and attention. The Korean Pentecost of 1907, DL Moody, The First Great Awakening 1727-50, George Whitfield, David Brainerd, The Second Great Awakening 1780-1810, The Cane Ridge Revival (1800) Aimee Simple McPhersen, Maria Woodworth-Etter, John G. Lake, Smith Wigglesworth…and the list goes on and on…like I said…mountains of books…And I love them all! I will also make sure at the end of *Unstoppable & Unquenchable Fire* to add some recommended reading for the burning hearts.

Through the lives of these ordinary men and women, and so many others, their journeys bore witness of the testimony of Jesus through supernatural exploits. These firebrands were the carriers and catalysts that changed their world. Presently, a new breed of pioneers is courageously and zealously advancing His victory in the demonstration and power of the Holy Spirit. With all my heart, I truly believe we are moving into a Third Great Awakening, which for the last 40 years, the Lord has lovingly and graciously prepared me!

God Loves America! He has not abandoned us, and His Hope for our Nation has not diminished nor withered. His hope is alive, burning and pulsating with everlasting Love. He is the Everlasting and Ever Faithful One. He is the Covenant keeping God. America is a special treasure to The Lord. She has been a catalyst to spread the knowledge of the Gospel of Jesus Christ to the earth, and now she must once again awaken to the Voice of God! My resolve is to do whatever I must, at any cost, to call our Nation back to God! My commitment is to ignite holy fire into this company of Kingdom reformers and agents of change to transform *the land of the free and the home of the brave* with the fire of God's Love!

It is no secret that we are living in unprecedented times of wickedness, idolatry, corruption, strife, confusion, compromise, deception, sexual sin and moral decadence. Without revival and a spiritual awakening transforming our Nation, America will implode into the worst apostasy we have ever seen. With that said, I am *not* a messenger of despair but of burning HOPE. I see an awakening and revival from the Carolinas to California…from the Beaches of Florida to the mountains of Alaska! Though I am deeply patriotic, I'm not talking about a red, white and blue revival, but a sweeping heaven sent reformation full of God's grace and truth!

I have not set out to give historical and linear perspective to past movements and awakenings, but rather I have set the course of this book to share what God's Holy fire does to envelope and shape our present world. To the man or woman that fully surrenders and yields to this all-consuming flame of Love, to them He gives the privilege and the power to fashion earth *as it is in heaven*. May The Spirit of God woo you into the courts of The Burning One where lightnings, thunders and blazing lamps dance before His holiness.

I pray that, as you read this book, The Spirit of God will light your heart and soul with holy fire. I have prayed that I will be able to effectively convey through His Spirit some of my personal experiences that will impart life, and lead you into a greater encounter with His burning Love. I pray that you will fully give yourself over to His divine purpose for you. I dare you to spend your whole life, affections, and resources pursuing the heart and face of God. He is worthy! If you dare to pledge your life to hosting His Presence and bringing the Presence of God into your world, then God will dedicate Himself to bringing you into your destiny!

I pray that you will be strengthened in your personal faith journey as you read through *Unstoppable and Unquenchable Fire*. I have prayed for those who will open these pages to experience a fresh encounter from the Lord and be saturated under the deluge of His affections towards you. I pray you laugh with tears of joy. I also pray you experience great tears of brokenness in His Presence. My desire is that fresh fire from heaven will consume your heart for God.

Our God is a consuming fire. The fire of His love is not of this world. There is no power in the known or unknown universe that can match the infinite glory and the majesty of The Great I AM! He is Pure Love. He is Holy Passion. He is All Powerful, All Knowing, Unrelenting, Unlimited, Irrefutable, Boundless, Infinite and Matchless in every way! He is Sovereign and Supreme! He cannot be contained in the heavens or in the earth! My prayer for you is that He will envelop and consume you in His burning Love and that you will become a catalyst of His burning heart to this generation and those that are yet to come!

JESUS is Unstoppable & Unquenchable Fire!
Brian Gibbs
A Messenger of Hope
Summer, 2014

CHAPTER ONE

OUT OF DARKNESS & INTO THE LIGHT

Colossians 1:13-14
"He has delivered us from the power of darkness and conveyed us into the kingdom of the Son of His love, in whom we have redemption through His blood, the forgiveness of sins".

ROCK N' ROLL – These are my earliest memories of growing up in the Gibbs' house with my Mom & Dad. My father (David) was a rock n' roll drummer in a band with his five brothers and some other wild friends. Hot lights, loud speakers, fog machines, wild crowds and chaos, alcohol and drugs – it was all a sure recipe for a family meltdown.

Music is our family gift. It seems everyone in the extended Gibbs family plays instruments, writes songs and just loves to rock! I started playing drums around age 3. Naturally, I gravitated towards them from watching and listening to Dad. My gift emerged quickly in me. Dad says that by the time I was 6, I was a better player than he. His band had me on stage early on, performing drum solos and shocking the crowds. I remember a night when one of my uncles took off my ball cap and began to pass it through the club during my solo time. They knew how to receive an offering!

I remember growing up in nightclubs around my family and the wild and intoxicated people. Elton John was right when he wrote the famous song, "Rocket Man"... "*Bars aren't the kind of place to raise your kids...in fact it's cold as hell and there's no one to raise them if you did*". It's true. Bars and clubs are not the kind of place you want to grow up. Even so, I always felt pretty safe in the clubs, even around the *crazies*, because I was confident my Dad and my uncles could take anyone out back and take care of business, if you know what I mean. Violence was just part of the package of the rock n' roll lifestyle.

(*Now before we move forward, this is NOT the story of The GIBB family known as The *BeeGees* – I don't want to ruin this book by having to talk about DISCO..haha...but you'd be surprised how many people have asked me time and again – *are you related to the BeeGees*? NOPE!) The good news is, if you like disco and tight shiny disco pants, Jesus still loves you! Enough said.

My Dad, along with his five brothers, loved to rock, and they worked hard at it. They were always found practicing, rehearsing and learning new songs - and tinkering to perfect their fire blasts of pyrotechnics! Even though they fought over differing ideas, they would always *kiss and make up*, so to speak. Now that's funny because in the 70's they connected with Paul Stanley and Gene Simmons to try and grow their bands' portfolio. But that's a whole other crazy story. If you don't know who "KISS" is, it's ok. Perhaps it's even better for you. Just keep reading.

Our house, porches, driveways and yards were always filled with music. The Beatles, Kiss, Rush, and Montrose were house favorites in those days. My Mom & Dad met young in life. Mom was 13 and Dad was 16 when they quickly fell in love with each other. They loved to party together and run around with their wild friends. Dad was a tough guy and drove muscles cars. He enjoyed martial arts, alcohol and immersed himself in the music, drugs and rebellious lifestyle of the 60's & 70's. Dad and his brothers grew up in terrible poverty along the Illinois River - with rats in the house, dirt floors and very little of anything. Abuse and poverty reigned in the family. In fact, my Mom was the first one to "groom" my dad; she gave his first toothbrush when he was 16. Sadly my grandparents had no parenting skills whatsoever as they tried to raise their 6 boys. I mean them absolutely no dishonor; it's just the truth. Dad's education was quite challenging because he couldn't read. The teachers gave him oral exams and just passed him along the system. He dropped out his junior year of high school, taking his first major job at Pabst Brewery. Dad would never return to school again. He was trying to make his own way after being kicked out by his parents because of recklessness. Alcohol had already taken my Grandfather into its grip and now it was trying to secure its stronghold in my Dad's life as well. In addition to lack of grooming, poverty and abuse, Dad had never been to church or known anything about Jesus or the Gospel.

My Mother, Karen, was raised with her three sisters in a much quieter Norwegian family atmosphere. They were not the rock n' roll type, just simple conservative Lutherans. Her father, Donavan Peck, fought in WWII, came home riddled by war and later became an alcoholic, but was later set free. Mom's family life was consistent and practical, but soon she met my dad, became enveloped by his life, and they ran at a fast pace.

Mom was a senior in high school when she became pregnant with me. In January 1973, Roe v Wade was passed in America. This brought into law the ability to abort a baby. I am forever grateful that my Mother never made this an option but considered my purpose to be precious and valuable. She gave me life! It's literally unfathomable to comprehend that in 40 years more than *55 Million* babies have been aborted in the United States of America. It's diabolical and iniquitous! I will share more about this later.

Being pregnant was not easy for my mom. It was stressful! However, her parents were very supportive. Being age 17 and riding the school bus home, she wondered what challenges life would bring her as she carried her baby. 1973 would shift her life forever. She walked the aisle and married Dad in March, graduated High School in May and in August gave birth to me on a warm summer night in Pekin, Illinois.

Nearly seven years into their marriage, life was spinning out of control. There was no joy in their lives or with each other - only pain, anger, regrets and darkness. As their marriage was coming apart at the seams, my Dad's very best friend was tragically murdered. Dad's decision to remain in a nightclub that night with my mom, most likely and miraculously, kept him from a premature death as well. The death of his friend took my Dad over the edge – his life got scary and dark. He plummeted into depression - contemplating his own life's purpose, his failing marriage and his unending torment from a wounded heart. Dad was violent and unpredictable. He wasn't able to keep any kind of consistent job. Alcohol was his faithful vice and hiding place. The hard excessive lifestyle of partying, drugs and alcohol had taken so much from my folks. It was destroying all the love they had.

In the midst of this chaos, my Dad somehow, and he would say miraculously, landed a job on a construction site with N.E. Finch, operating heavy equipment and stacking steel for Caterpillar during their strike in 1979. *I know what you're thinking - Wow, an alcoholic/drug user operating heavy equipment?* I know, it's so ridiculous! Can you believe it? However, he was a certified crane operator. Little did my Dad know that he was about to come into the presence of a man who walked with God and knew God intimately!

A Divine Invasion of Privacy

Dad had been on the job for about three weeks loading the steel, but he was miserable and trying to figure out his life and his marriage. When he started there, the men on the site warned him about the strange Foreman – a 6'2 African American named Miles Black. They warned my Dad that the Foreman/Union Steward was a *Preacher Man*. He seemed odd to my Dad. Understand that, as a crane operator, Dad had to watch him constantly all day long. It was critical for Miles to give him arm signals to assist with the crane placement in moving the steel. What was curious from a distance, my Dad could see Miles' lips moving constantly, as if he were talking to himself. Little did he know, Miles was interceding for his life.

I think it's critical that I bring something to the surface for you to understand. God was inserting His friend, Miles, into my Dad's work environment to bring heaven into the Gibbs Family. There were other demonic strongholds in our family besides poverty, alcohol, sexual sins and drugs – there was a deeply prejudicial spirit and a thick hatred for Blacks. I do not want to go into great detail about my family's heritage in the Ku Klux Klan (KKK), except to say it was very real, very dark and present in my generational line. When God brought Miles Black into our world, you couldn't get any "blacker" than Miles Black! I know that's not good English, but you get the point! God was ready to lay His ax of Love to the roots of demonic strongholds in my family. The Holy Spirit's intention to purge iniquity from my family was relentless and He had destined to set us upon the immoveable Rock of Ages. Remember, His Love is unstoppable and He will not relent until He has you completely!

While Dad worked these three weeks at the construction site, he would come home each night only to fight time and again with my Mother about their imploding marriage and misery. She had enough and was finally at the end. They resolved to divorce one another. My Mom had the divorce papers officially drawn up at the Courthouse and they agreed to meet the next day at noon to sign the papers together. The plan was for Mom and me to move out to live at her Parents' home. I was devastated. I knew at six years old what was happening. I knew they weren't happy, and at times our house was a scary place. I knew we were being torn apart. I wanted them to love each other and stay together, even in the madness and chaos. Mom told me what the plan was going to be and how we would live permanently this time with Grandpa and Grandma. I was nervous and full of fear.

This night would change everything! Dad had come home from work and they talked through the process of the divorce and the plans for us moving out the next day, after everything was settled at the Courthouse. Later into the night, Mom and I were out in the front room together and I wanted to go and talk to Dad. He was laying alone on their bed. I went in and shut the door behind me. I was just a boy. But, I was crushed, broken and did not want us to leave. I was crying. I didn't want to live with Grandpa and Grandma Peck. I wanted us to stay together. I layed across my Dad's chest and pleaded with him not to send us away. I told him I didn't like what was happening. In his own way, he tried to comfort and strengthen me. He told me that everything would be ok and that things would work out better for all of us. Finally, he peeled me off his chest and asked me to leave the room, as he needed to go to bed and head out early for work in the morning.

I got up off of my Dad, turned towards the door, and as I reached for the door handle an amazing Presence came upon me. I did not know what or Who it was. It was Present – around me, on me– tangible – I could feel it. I turned towards my Dad, and he sat up in bed looking at me strangely. I wondered if he was feeling what I was feeling. Suddenly, I said to him – *"Dad, God wants me to say something to you! Dad, God wants me to say something to you!"* His response was; *"Say it, Brian"*. I spoke as an adult with authority, strength and compassion. And these were the words; *"Dad, God is telling me to tell you that you will never find true happiness in this life, until you give your life to JESUS CHRIST. He is what you are looking for. All of the drugs, all of your running around that you are doing... you will never find true happiness in this life until you give your life to JESUS. And Dad, if you don't give your life to Jesus soon, you will die and go to Hell."* I turned around, opened the door, ran down the hallway into the living room and sat on the couch, thinking about what I had just said to him. I knew what I said, but I didn't know what it meant because I had not been to church or heard the Gospel. I was thinking about the Presence I felt in his bedroom. It lingered upon me. It was warm, comforting and strong. I never said a word to my Mom about what happened and fell asleep on the couch.

The next morning, Dad left early for the construction site. His plan was to get off early so he could sign the divorce papers at noon.

When he arrived, he was met by Miles Black. After a brief talk about the work plan for the day, he climbed into his crane and began to move the steel. My words from the night before haunted him. He was seeing his entire relationship with my Mother and with me crumble to nothing. He was broken and confused. The morning break came at 10:15am that morning, and while on break Miles walked up to my Dad and said; *"Dave, I have message for you"*. Knowing that Miles was his Foreman, he was concerned that he was going to get fired. Not only was he losing his marriage, his wife and child, but now he was going to be losing his job. My Dad asked, *"Who's the message from?"* Miles response was, *"The message is from GOD"*! My Dad said; *"Really, well what does God have to say to me, Mr. Preacher Man?* Miles said, *"Did you listen to what your little boy said last night in your bedroom?"* My Dad was stunned and gasped! Miles said again; *"Dave, did you listen to what your little boy said last night in your bedroom? Dave, I've been praying for you every day since you came on this job site. Last night as I was praying, God gave me an open vision of your bedroom. I saw your son walk into your room crying that he didn't want to leave. And, Dave, before he left your room he turned and this is what he said."* He told my Dad word for word what I said the night before! And then Miles said; *"Your son is right, Dave, if you don't give your life to Jesus soon you will die and go to hell"*. Then he turned and walked away from my Dad. Dad was overwhelmed and completely bewildered! These questions kept racing through his mind; *How did that man know what happened in our house last night? How did he know what Brian said? How did he know such things?*

Ladies and gentlemen, there is a GOD that loves YOU! His Love is an unstoppable, unquenchable fire!

When Dad left work that day, he didn't go to the Courthouse to meet Mom and to sign the papers. Instead, he went home and locked himself in his room. He didn't know what to think. He was overcome. He was thinking of what it meant to die and go to Hell. He was thinking of his friend that had been murdered…Where was he? Is eternity real? How did that man know what happened in his bedroom? How did he know everything Brian had said? He stayed locked in his room and he made a commitment that day to not sign any papers. My Mom was upset that he had not shown up at the courthouse. Yet, out of curiosity, we did not move out that night. We stayed home.

The next morning, Miles met Dad for the morning break, sat him down and began to talk with him about Jesus. My Dad was 27 years old. This was the first time he had ever heard the Gospel! Armed with a little pocket New Testament that he carried with him, Miles took the time to read the Word of God to my Dad and reveal who JESUS is. Day by day, this went on for weeks. Mom and I had no idea what was happening. Dad went to work. Miles went to work too, but in a new way! He was working the works of God. As he shared more and more of the glorious love of God, Miles made it clear that God had sent His only begotten Son to save the world – more to the point, to save my Dad! Each day, Dad would come home and stay back in his room. His countenance and behavior was different. We didn't know why, and we dared not ask him. I was happy we didn't move out to Grandpa and Grandma's house.

After weeks of Miles sharing the Gospel, Dad asked him, in some general way, a question that summed everything up. "What do I need to do with all of this, Miles?" His response is still baffling, because if someone asked me how to be saved, I'd be ready to take them through a prayer of repentance and so on and so forth...but Miles simply said to my Dad, "*You'll know what to do, Dave*". It was November 27th, 1979. At about 3:30am, my Dad got out of bed and fell to his knees. Not knowing how to *officially pray*, he just started weeping before God, talking about his life to God and sharing how much of a mess it was. He asked Jesus to come into His life and be His Savior and Lord! My Dad encountered the Love of God in the most supernatural way that night. He wept. He laughed. He worshipped. Dad was *born again*!

The next morning when Dad arrived on the site, Miles was there to meet him and celebrate my Dad's new birth, loving on him in such a profound way! Dad had just started living!

Soon, my Mom was wondering what had happened to Dad. She was puzzled and a little freaked out that each day found him home after work. His presence was clearly far from the norm. Something major was different, fresh and new. One night, she asked him, *"Dave, what has happened to you"?* He responded, *"Karen, I'm saved...I got saved"!* Perplexed, she responded, *"Saved from what?"* That night, Dad took Mom through the whole unfolding of grace. He told her how I had come into their bedroom the night before they were going to sign "the papers". He told her what I had said, and how that the next day Miles Black told him word for word everything that had happened in the bedroom. Mom heard the Gospel that night and she made the greatest decision of her life at 24 years of age. She opened her heart to be consumed by the Love of God! That night, Mom's response was perfect. She told my Dad, *"I want to be SAVED too".* Dad led my Mom to The Lord! She was his first convert.

How beautiful is that? Two kids growing up together, trying to find their way through the haze and noise of life, only to have GOD invade their world!

Dad invited Miles to come to our home in Pekin to share more of the Gospel with him and my Mom. Beyond working construction, Miles was pastoring a church in the south side of Peoria. Our hometown in those days was especially known for its deep prejudice against Blacks and its KKK network. Asking Miles to come to our home during the night to share the Word with us was a dangerous request, but out of love, Miles came for nearly two months and imparted The Gospel into my folks. He soon encouraged them to find a good church where they could grow. He encouraged them that Holy Spirit would lead them where to go. I really love that! Miles knew and trusted Holy Spirit. I'm thankful he didn't try to control them or heavily persuade them to attend a specific church.

Soon after, we went and visited a little Baptist Church in our town. It had an organ, a pulpit and a few pews. That first morning, Mom and Dad dropped me off in a Sunday School class. As the teacher began to share Jesus, it was then that revelation came into my young heart. This was The JESUS that I had told my Dad about in his bedroom. As the teacher shared the Gospel, I felt that same Presence! Faith came alive in me, and I knew Jesus was real! When the teacher asked who desired to open their heart to Jesus and make Him their Lord and Savior, I lifted my hand and went forward and received Christ into my life! I will never forget that day.

Holy Spirit | Tongues, Fire, Deliverance & Bliss

Mom was reading the Scriptures to us at home. (Remember, Dad couldn't read). We had made our way through the Gospels and came to the amazing **Book of Acts**. As Mom read through the first few Chapters, we were completely blown away by what we were hearing and feeling. Desire began to burn inside of them for this infilling – this *baptism of Holy Spirit*. Mom and Dad had a desire for power in their lives to overcome the vices that were still lingering. They were clearly saved, but they were under conviction of their lifestyle and habits that held them and they wanted real freedom. The more they read, the more excited they became. In childlike faith, they simply made up their minds that they had to have this "Holy Spirit stuff" – this "Fire" and "Speaking in tongues". With great anticipation we headed off for the little Baptist Church the next week, and my Dad couldn't wait to talk to the Pastor about Holy Spirit, as he desired this encounter for himself and his family. After Church that morning, Dad approached the pastor with the Scriptures open to Acts and asked the Pastor about the baptism of the Holy Spirit. His question was met with fierce resistance. All at once, the Pastor said to my Dad, "Come with me right now". He led my Dad to his office, shut the door behind him and told my Dad; "*That Holy Spirit stuff – speaking in tongues, well, it's of the devil and if you talk to anyone in the Church about speaking in tongues we're going to kick you out*" (along with other condescending remarks). Dad was shocked and his spirit was grieved. He told the Pastor there would be no need to kick us out...and that we would be on our way. Forrest Gump said, "*stupid is, as stupid does.*" Miles had told my Dad that, "If it's in The Book, you can have it too! " That advice helped us make a quick transition and our exit.

I want to be clear here to say that I love our Baptist brothers and sisters in the Lord. What that misled "*minister*" said to my Dad doesn't define what all Baptists believe. Nonetheless, this was our experience and our experience clearly does not define The Baptist Church.

Mom and Dad were greatly discouraged. They were hungry for more of God in their lives and they desired to experience Him in power. Remember this friend; God knows your address! He knows how and where to find you!

Mom and I were at the house a few weeks later watching a television broadcast called, "It's A Miracle". Interestingly, Dad was at his brother Mike's home watching the same program. The Program was from a local church in town called First Assembly. The Pastor was sharing a fresh miracle story about a little boy in the church who had a disease, which was causing the child's lungs to lose function. One lung had already been destroyed and the other was deteriorating quickly. The Church remained in fasting and prayer for many weeks - the family praying in the hospital. Then, God gave this baby two brand new lungs! Yes, that's right! Two brand new lungs! Whoa! This was a live broadcast. When the camera panned over to the boy's father, who was being interviewed, he was introduced as Rev. Jim Carrington. My Dad was in shock to find that this was a guy he had known. He thought Jim had died in Vietnam. The hotline opened that night for calls and Mom called in to find information about the Church. Soon after her call, Dad arrived home and before she could get the words out of her mouth about the TV program she had just seen, my Dad started telling us that he had seen a miracle story on a television program at Mike's house and wanted to call the hotline. Can you say *divine convergence*? As Dad called in, he spoke to one of the associate Pastors and shared that he knew Jim Carrington, and that he and my Mom had recently gotten saved and were looking for a church that believed in the God of miracles. Guess where we went to church a few days later? Yep...that's right.

We showed up at First Assembly that Sunday. It wasn't like the little Baptist Church with the organ, pulpit and a few pews. The parking lot was packed, the church was packed and I remember walking into the Sanctuary...Wow! People were singing, filled with joy, lifting their hands...they had a full praise and worship band. There were no colored lights and fog machines like the clubs, but they had a band - in Church! And we were excited. Above all, what was most significant was The Presence in that place. It was thick and tangible. After the service, Jim approached our family to get reacquainted and introduce us to the Lead Pastor. My Dad was ready with his question. He asked the Pastor, *Do you believe in the Holy Spirit and the baptism of the Spirit and speaking in tongues?* The Pastor answered, "*Yes we sure do! Why don't you come back tonight; I'm going to be bringing a message on this.*" Mom and Dad lit up. And yes, you guessed it - we were there that night! READY!

The Pastor preached like a man on fire. He was sharing out of the Book of Acts the wonder of Holy Spirit coming to fill mankind. Near the end of his message he gave an altar call – an open invitation for those who desired to be filled with The Holy Spirit. My Dad didn't know there was altar "protocol" so to speak. He ran to the front and began pleading with the Pastor. He desired this! The Pastor quickly gathered some men and elders for my Dad, but before they could pray for him, Dad ran back and grabbed my Mom to bring her to the altar as well. The women took my Mom to one side of the stage and the men took Dad to the other, and they began to pray over them. It was quite a sight. Within minutes, Dad was immersed in the fire of The Lord - he was filled to overflowing and speaking in tongues with joy and weeping! Mom on the other hand was…well…nothing was happening.

We left the Church that night pretty late. Dad was lit up and Mom was sorely disappointed and struggling to find answers why she didn't receive. On the way home we swung into the grocery store to grab a few things. Mom and I were in the canned foods isle and Dad…well, Dad was somewhere in the store…kind of…he was in another realm. This is just how it happened. Mom bent down to pick up a can of Pork n' Beans and suddenly she was baptized in the Holy Spirit and began speaking in tongues! Oh my! Dad found us as heaven was invading our family right in the grocery store. We made it out of the store and got back to the house. That night something significant happened! Not only were my parents filled with the Holy Spirit, but they were completely and utterly delivered from drugs and alcohol! The chains of addiction and affliction were destroyed! There was a thorough house cleaning as all things were becoming new!

The next day, Dad was outside in a lawn chair while I was in the driveway playing. He heard a voice in his heart that told him to go and get the book that he and Mom had received at First Assembly. It was the Gospel of John and a simple book to help new converts and those who had just been filled with the Holy Spirit. My Dad was wrestling with the notion of going to get the book. After all, he couldn't read. Finally, after hearing *"Go Get The Book"* three or four times, he was finally obedient and went into the house to find it. He snuck out of the house with the book, not wanting my Mom to see him with it, and sat back down in his lawn chair. He opened the book and suddenly began to READ! *"In the beginning was the Word, and the Word was with God, and the Word was God. He was in the beginning with God. All things were made through Him, and without Him nothing was made that was made. In Him was life, and the life was the light of men. And the light shines in the darkness, and the darkness did not comprehend it..."* Each night Mom read the Scriptures to Dad. But that night, Dad had a big surprise for her. He interrupted her and said, "Let me read it now." He took the Bible and began to read to her. She was so astonished that she began to weep! We had Church that night in the Gibbs' house! God's favor can restore in a day what was stolen over a lifetime. Who is like our God? There is no one!

A few weeks later, I too answered the call and went to the altar to receive The Holy Spirit. I can still remember right where I was kneeling in First Assembly. There was a large woman in the Church that everyone affectionately called "Sister Jean". At 7 years of age, I was terrified of her. Every time I saw her in the church coming my way I would get nervous. But that night, I was kneeling and praying and asking Jesus to fill me with The Holy Spirit, like he filled my Mom and Dad. I was earnestly pressing in, and then a hand touched me on my back. I looked behind me and was shocked to see "Sister Jean"!!! She said in a sweet and compassionate voice, *"Your seeking the Holy Spirit aren't you, Son?"* I nodded my head. And she said, *"Just open your heart to*

Jesus and you're about to receive right now". The moments following were bliss! I was trembling (not because I was terrified of Jean) but I was trembling and weeping because I was immersed in Pure Love and filled to overflowing with His Presence - speaking in heavenly tongues. It was a defining moment in my life – fire and love!

First Assembly became our new family and life was changing rapidly for the Gibbs. We were growing in the knowledge of the Word, baptized in water and connecting to a spirit-filled community. We were learning what it really means to worship and encounter God's Presence in a corporate gathering. People were being saved all around us and baptized in The Holy Spirit. We were being discipled in a home fellowship group from our Church with The Carrington family – the family in which God healed the little boy's lungs. It was a hopping place!

Our house had a new and clean atmosphere. The thick darkness and depression was gone and Holy Spirit was showing up and showing off! Dad was filling it up with new music – Keith Green, Dallas Holm, 2nd Chapter of Acts, Phil Keaggy, Petra, Don Francisco, The Imperials, BJ Thomas and many more. I must have heard Keith Green's song, *"Love Broke Through"*, a thousand times in those days. During this time of transformation, another glorious gift was given to our family with the birth of my brother, Joey, in 1980. He was a bundle of pure joy and not surprisingly, he was born with *rockstar* hair that stood straight up in all directions and refused to lie down!

That summer, there was a terrible drought in the Midwest. The Illinois River's watermark was at a record low. We lived right on the River. The only thing between us and it were the railroad tracks up on the levy. We lived three blocks north of the Pekin bridge and the River flows south. Remember that, because it's notable for this particular story.

Late one summer night, my brother Joey and I were in the room that we shared. Our bedroom was in the back of the house and Dad always left the back porch light on. I looked out the window and saw something moving and ran into their bedroom to tell my folks that someone or something was out back. Dad was up and out the back door in a flash. To his surprise there was someone standing there not far from the porch light. When he pulled the person into the light to get a better look, he realized it was a woman literally covered from head to toe in thick river mud! Dad quickly pulled her into the house, sat her down in the kitchen and had Mom call the police. He kept asking if she was alright and who she was. The woman seemed to be in a state of shock. She was hardly able to talk. My Dad kept questioning her. "What happened to you?" "Where did you come from?"

Finally, the woman said that she tried to kill herself! She was running away from a broken relationship and she planned to take her own life. She was on the other side of the river driving as fast as she could along the road leading to the bridge. With intention, she drove her car into a cornfield flipping it over and over again. Though it was demolished, she remained uninjured. She climbed out of the wreckage and walked out onto the road. She had made the decision to walk up onto the bridge, and try again. She would remove her shoes and jump off. Remember, there was a terrible drought and the Illinois River was extremely low. She said that she reached the top of the bridge, took of her shoes and placed them on the ledge. She jumped off, hit the water, opened her eyes and she was standing at our back door, looking at a sign my Dad had hung by the porch light that read, *"As For Me & My House, We Shall Serve The Lord"* (Joshua 24:15)

We were shocked! There she sat - soaking wet and covered in thick, thick, thick river mud. How did she get to our house? By this time, the police had arrived and were standing in our kitchen observing the interactions. Dad took this as an obvious sign of God's providence and led this woman to Jesus! Soon after the cops took her away, Mom called into the police station to check on how she was doing. The Officer said, *"We just found her car in the cornfield and her shoes up on the bridge just as she had said."*

We lived three blocks north of the Pekin bridge and the river flows south. Imagine if the river would have been at its regular watermark! She most likely would have hit the water and her dead body would have eventually washed up miles down south. But she hit the water, when the river was at its lowest and plummeted into the riverbed. I believe angels picked this precious young woman up and carried her three blocks north of the bridge to the Gibbs' house to be introduced to her Savior – JESUS!

You may feel stuck in the mud, so to speak, right now in your life. But I pray that the supernatural power of The Holy Spirit will pick you up, clean you off and restore life to you as you journey with me in this book.

The woman from the bridge was only the beginning of supernatural anomalies that God started bringing to us. Wave after wave of troubled people - desperate and without hope in their lives - seemed to supernaturally find their way to our door. Like battered ships, they were drawn to a lighthouse. We began to see real and profound miracles.

Dad quickly became a powerhouse soul-winner! He was leading men to the Lord everywhere he went, telling his testimony of Grace and how God invaded his life and marriage! He experienced this unstoppable fire and he told everyone he could about Jesus! Soon, our Pastor Ron Callahan interviewed Dad on "It's A Miracle", asking about his transformation and about winning souls and loving the *unlovable*.

Through some supernatural events, a Mission Center called *Jesus Today Outreach*, in downtown Peoria, was in need of a new director. Dad was asked to take the position. The "job" was about winning souls – loving the homeless, the broken, runaways and the needy. It was through this ministry opportunity that my Mom and Dad's spiritual trajectory soared, as they served in the streets of Peoria.

The compassions of Jesus were filling my Dad. He was in the streets, in the alleyways, under the bridges, in the cardboard boxes, outside the clubs – fearlessly preaching and winning people to Christ. His salary was meager at best at the Outreach. But, while Dad was in the streets, Mom worked very hard in her office jobs to provide and make a home for us. Little by little, we made our way.

Dad built a small volunteer staff - that was just as possessed by Love as him. They started traveling with dad to hold community outreach services throughout the region in churches, parks and community centers. Dad had our worship teams coming over from the Church in Pekin, and started inviting ministry friends to come and speak on the weekends at the Outreach. Soon, our Church family and other churches were coming to serve from everywhere, just to be a part of this outreach.

People were profoundly meeting Jesus – salvations, healings and deliverances were a way of life. Teams were being equipped to go out on the streets and preach and pray for the sick. It was raw ministry - real and compassionate - Jesus with no gimmicks and no supplements added. Pastor Callahan had taught my Dad well; that *JESUS is the same yesterday, today and forever* (Hebrews 13:8). *What He did in the streets of Israel over 2000 years ago, He could do today in the streets of Central Illinois!* I'm forever grateful for Pastor Callahan loving my family and becoming a spiritual father to my Mom & Dad. Without his love, leadership and extraordinary gift of preaching the Word, we would have become roaming gypsies in the Kingdom of God.

This cultural kaleidoscopic, called *Jesus Today Outreach,* is where Jesus took great joy in breaking my heart for the lost! These lost and lonely souls had absolutely nothing. They came in from every-where - runaways, hitch hikers, homeless vagabonds - wanderers looking for hope and a reason to live. They found Jesus there, or perhaps He found them. It affected me deep inside. Dad's team had their hands full. They had to deal with every scenario imagin-able, patiently caring for hardened hearts and fearlessly confront-ing the powers of darkness and casting out devils.

Dad started bringing colorful homeless friends to our house for the holidays. We would feed them, clothe them and provide a warm bath. It had its challenges, but I'm forever grateful that Mom and Dad opened our home to them. I don't know how their hospital-ity changed those men throughout the years, but it changed me. And it awakened me to the ugly realities of life and to the beautiful power of love. I remember one year when Mom and Dad brought one of our homeless friends (Henry) over for the holidays, and Dad had him spend the night. Henry slept under the Peoria Bridge in a cardboard box, and Dad often joined him there, with candles during the winters and loved on him. Joey was upset that Dad made him sleep in my room, so that our guest could sleep in Joey's room. I'm not sure if Joey ever recovered from Henry urinating in his bed that night - fond memories of giving and practical love. Or, perhaps it's a fond memory because my bed stayed dry. Well, you get the point.

A Call To Ministry

Each year, our Church would host camps for both elementary aged kids, as well as for family. First Assembly had an old campground just outside of town where they bused hundreds of kids. The chapel had sawdust floors and old wooden benches. It was quite a place...a place I grew to love. The grounds were beautiful with hills for hiking, thick woods and creeks. I went every year for kids' camp and also our Holy Spirit Camp Meetings, which our Church likewise hosted.

For Junior & Senior High we would travel each summer down to Carlinville, Illinois for a statewide camp, hosting thousands of students. This particular year would become a defining moment, as God called me into the ministry! I was thirteen, and my life vision was to become a rock n' roll drummer. Well, a *Christian*, rock n' roll drummer that is! I had grandiose dreams of becoming the next Robert Sweet from Stryper, with a mega double bass drum to take the Gospel to the masses through Rock! At 41 years old it makes me laugh. Pretty lofty, right? But at thirteen, growing up in my family, it just made perfect sense!

God had a greater vision for my life than I did. I remember the night so well. Sam Farina was the camp speaker that year and I loved Sam. He was one of my favorite speakers at First Assembly for the prayer and revival meetings, which Pastor Callahan hosted for our region. Sam preached powerfully and passionately that night. He gave a specific charge and challenged us to answer the call of God on our lives and commit ourselves to His divine plan and design. Like hundreds of kids that night, I made my way down to the altar. I remember kneeling before the Lord against the stage and asking God to use my life to make a difference; I wanted to be His friend and partner. As I was kneeling before the Lord, I heard Him. It wasn't audible, but it was deep in my spirit. He told me he had a special plan for my life and showed me that he would make me a gift to the Body of Christ. Later that night, I went into *orbit* (so to speak) as hands were placed upon me, I laid in the altar area for quite some time committing my path, my plans, my future unto The Lord. Later that year God branded my young heart with Jeremiah 3:15, *"And I will give you shepherds according to My heart, who will feed you with knowledge and understanding."*

When God shared this with Jeremiah, it was as if God was literally quoting Himself concerning what He had spoken about a young man, David, who became the King of Israel. David's journey was far from perfection, but he pursued God relentlessly with his whole heart. God said of David, *"that he was a man after God's own heart"* (1 Samuel 13:14). God was true to that Word for my life. Not only did he raise up shepherds to feed and instruct me, but he would put me on a quest that would shape and groom me to become His shepherd and messenger according to His own heart.

Throughout my Junior High years and early into High School I had a notable dream over and over again. I dreamt that I would sneak out of my bedroom window late at night when everyone was sleeping and stand under the stars out in front of our home. Then I would run as fast as I could down the street, towards a massive cornfield that could be found at the end of our street. Like an airplane bolting down the runway, I ran as hard and as fast as I could. When I reached the cornfield I would be transformed into a mighty eagle soaring upward into the night sky. I would rise up over Illinois and begin to fly south over the US towards Florida. I flew over Nashville, then Atlanta and down the west coastline of Florida wrapping around the Keys to Miami. Next I would shoot up the Eastern Coast through Washington DC, New York, Boston and Maine. Then I would sweep across the Great Lakes to the other corner of the US, over Seattle and down through San Francisco to San Diego. Finally I made my way home through the western mountains, over Illinois and down to our street...would transform back into my 13 year old frame and run back to our house, climbing back through my window only to wake up and start the day. I had this same dream over and over for nearly three years. I didn't realize it at that time, but God was prophetically sharing a secret with me about my destiny and purpose. I will share later, in chapters ahead, how this dream would become a prophetic touchstone in the journey!

Yes, Yes...I know you're singing right now, *"I want to fly like an eagle to the sea...fly like an eagle let the Spirit carry me...I want to fly... oh yeah, fly right into the future"*...I love that song too! Hey, major kudos to The Steve Miller Band, but Seal's version of the song was the best from the mid 90's! Sorry, no time to argue that...Seal's is the best...ok, ok, done. Let's keep moving forward...Haha!

In my freshman year of High School our Church family was hit with some extremely big challenges. One of them was the removal of our Pastor. The loss of him and his family made for a very trying and difficult time. For those of you who have been in church anytime at all, you understand that the Church is not perfect. It is true that we are being perfected into His image and likeness, and yes, we are His Chosen Bride that is being cleansed from every blemish and stain, but sometimes people forget what Kingdom they're really from. The news of our Pastor leaving was a shocking blow to our entire region. It's baffling how men can be in close proximity, yet in any given situation, ready to rise and strike the shepherds with their own agenda. This was the case in the leadership of our Church. And frankly, seeing this in my adolescent years, it scared me. I would secretly say to the Lord in prayer, *Lord if they can do that to our Pastor, what could men do to me when I'm leading or Pastoring one day?*

In those years, God began to share His secrets with me about shepherds and the heart of a true shepherd. I knew my Pastor wasn't a perfect man, but Jesus was The Perfect Shepherd and he was killed for perfection. Mom, Dad and their closest friends in the Church were devastated. That is not an exaggeration whatsoever. I had never seen my Dad weep so intensely. Pastor Callahan was their spiritual Papa and so much more. People in the church behaved maliciously and dishonorably. It was grieving beyond words. One of the most notable things I remember throughout this time was how my Mom and Dad continued to honor our Pastor.

It was challenging to see people behaving so degradingly and destructively. The *enemy* was masquerading with lots of theatre, and sadly people became casualties to his deceit. There were rivers of unending tears as families began leaving the church. The erosion of hope was significant, as friend after friend were saying goodbye - their families leaving in search of another church. It broke our heart time and again. Hundreds of people left and were scattered in different churches, or worse, no church at all.

Interim pastors and itinerant ministers came and went. More of our friends were leaving with offense and unforgiveness. Mom and Dad navigated through much uncertainty. With prayer, they kept their hearts right with people and circumstance. They walked in love. Finally, Mom and Dad presented my brother and I with their decision to move on from the Church and find a new Church family. Those were some difficult and challenging years of transition through High School. Some of the men that had left the church started hosting their own meetings in town and eventually started churches that shut down within a year or two. They were good men with good intentions, but their attempts never took flight. Disappointment was settling into our home and it was evident in the faces of my parents. Dad tried to keep the fire burning at the Outreach, as he was resolved to keep moving forward. We were unhappy with how things were unfolding. Eventually, my parents let me go back to the Church to attend some youth functions and see old friends that had weathered through the changes.

The Winds of Change

By the time I entered my senior year in High School I was really wrestling with God's call on my life. I loved The Lord deeply and had a real relationship with Him, but I couldn't figure out how he was going to do anything worthwhile through my life, although I sure wanted Him to! I was insecure and had no confidence whatsoever in getting up to speak in front of any gathering, large or small. My family was experiencing turbulence and challenges on the inside. The Church situation was bleak and frustrating. I was disappointed at how things were unfolding, and I was praying for The Lord to direct my steps in preparing for ministry.

One Sunday morning, as I was back visiting at our old home church, a woman came over to me whom I had known for many years. She placed a brochure in my hand. It contained information about Southeastern Bible College in Florida. She had heard that I had gone up to Minneapolis to check out a Bible School there, and she thought perhaps I should take a look at Southeastern. I shared it with Mom and Dad and got their blessing to fly down a month later with a friend of mine.

Flying into Florida was like flying into a piece of heaven! It's not Illinois. I remember seeing the ocean for the first time from the plane window and getting excited about the possibility of life in Florida. I was ready for a fresh start, and I wanted to discover what God had in store for me. I immediately gravitated to the culture and atmosphere of the College. After three great days of experiencing classes, meeting students and teachers and walking the campus in prayer (& hitting the beach too), I felt this was going to be the right place for training.

In August of 1991, on my 18th Birthday, I started Bible College with a Pastoral/Evangelistic ministry emphasis. I started connecting well with students and friendships quickly forged. There were so many tremendous students from throughout the country who were pursuing God's call. It was an exciting time for me, a brand new chapter in life and I was ready to launch out! I was enjoying my studies, especially learning revival history. The more I read about historical outpourings of the Spirit and revival, the more my heart began to hunger for God and to experience His glory. I had a burning hunger and zeal for the Lord, and I believed that if I was privileged enough to be called His messenger then I too desired the promise of Psalm 104:4, "The Lord makes His messengers flames of fire." My prayer was that His holy fire would be unquenchable in me and demonstrated with His power! As the Apostle Paul wrote in his letters, "For the kingdom of God is not in word but in power" (1 Corinthians 4:20).

Meeting The Woman That Would
Forever Change My Life

One afternoon, as I was leaving the cafeteria and heading back to my dorm room, I heard this group of girls laughing and carrying on with one another. There was a beautiful brunette girl that immediately caught my eye. I watched her laughing and smiling with her friends, but she never saw me. I went back to my dorm and told The Lord, *I would really like to meet that girl!* Throughout the next several weeks I saw her time and again walking across the campus or into the cafeteria. One afternoon, I was in a class and realized that one of her friends from that group of girls, Amy, was sitting across from me. Amy was randomly talking about some of her friends, so I was listening in to maybe catch her name. I listened and wondered if she might be talking about that stunning brunette. I asked her about her brunette friend. And she replied, *"Her name is Brenda, but she has a boyfriend from Ohio, so don't even think about it!"* That was the end of the conversation. I never asked her another thing about Brenda (Bren), but I kept seeing her and eventually I started seeing her with her boyfriend from Ohio.

I was out walking the Campus and praying one afternoon, about a month later, and ran into Amy. She asked me what I was doing that night, and to my surprise she invited me to attend a surprise party for Bren. I was a little taken aback, but immediately I told her I would be there. I went back to my room and thought about my prayer...hmmm. Interesting! I made her a card and met up with the group for the party.

They were planning how to get Bren to the party without her knowing it was a surprise. One of the guys, Bruce, recommended that I come with him and get Bren from the Music Hall. Bruce thought it was perfect to bring me, because she didn't know who I was. That way, perhaps, she wouldn't expect anything. Moments later outside of the Music Hall I was introduced to Bren. Wow! She smiled, I shook her hand, and she spoke beautifully and gently. We went up into the Campus Café where everyone was waiting to surprise her. It was a fun night! I watched from a distance as her friends showered her with funny cards and gifts, and it was a joy to sit and watch her laugh. Oh yes, her boyfriend was there too, but hey, God was answering my prayers, and that's what is important right?

A few days later we saw each other and walked across campus together. A few after that, it happened again. Then a few days after that, it happened again. Are you seeing a pattern here? Soon, we were taking walks together around the College campus and the soccer fields. I enjoyed her company so much. The Presence of The Lord rested beautifully upon Bren, and I loved being with her. I loved her presence and her countenance. She was humble but carried herself with dignity.

For the next couple of months our friendship really developed. We shared our stories of growing up, our families, our goals and our calling. I felt so comfortable sharing with her. I was completely attracted to Bren from the moment I saw her, but honestly, I really wasn't hopeful that anything could happen between us. That's the truth, and not false humility. Her boyfriend was a good guy. I liked him, but I didn't think they were a "fit". It's funny thinking back on those days. There were times when we would be out for a walk, and she would let me know that she needed to get back to meet up with John for their date. I never brought up John in any of our conversations. We never talked about her dating him. One night, she tried to bring John up and talk about their dating. I simply said, *"Your relationship with John is none of my business."*

Late in my freshman year, I met a great guy named Rusty Nelson who was already a graduate and overseeing the Alumni program from Southeastern. Rusty and his wife Leisa were also dynamic worship leaders at a church in town called Carpenter's Home. Together they led teams from the college, doing special outreaches across the country. They were in need of a drummer for their worship team. Rusty had gotten word about me from a mutual friend and we connected on campus. Soon I was taking trips and playing the drums for his worship team on the road and enjoying the evangelistic outreaches. They were raw and passionate and reminded me of my Dad's team from the *Jesus Today Outreach* days.

In my sophomore year at Southeastern, I remember running into Bren on one of our first days back to school. It was right near the area where we first met. It was wonderful to see her and hear her voice again. It was good to reconnect…and yes, she was still dating John. Interestingly enough, we found out that we had a class together. Can you believe it? It was "Marriage & Family". Hmmm… more on that later.

About two months later, I met a lovely girl from Florida named Megan. She was a Junior with an Education major studying to be a teacher. A mutual friend had introduced us, and we hit it off right away. Within the first few months of dating her, I told her about my friendship with Bren. What was strange (or maybe it was God), was while I started dating Megan, we would often see Bren and John out around town too. Lakeland has lots of beautiful parks and lakes to enjoy, as long as you look out for the alligators. I remember one particular day that Megan and I were out enjoying a drive and who did we see? Yep, you guessed it, Bren and John lying on a blanket by the lake talking, taking in some premium Florida sunshine and watching the swans. It was weird, and I thought to myself, *"Those two don't belong together…they're just wasting their time."* Unfortunately, I should have been looking harder into my own relationship with Megan with prayer and discernment rather than judging Bren.

Marriage & Family class was interesting and frankly was getting a touch more challenging. You see, I was dating Megan but kept gravitating towards Bren. I was frustrated with the feelings I was experiencing. A few months later, I saw Bren at the campus café, and she asked me how it was going with Megan. I was reluctant to talk to her about our relationship, so I kept the conversation pretty shallow. Bren felt like Megan and I didn't belong together, but she stayed quiet about her feelings and what she was discerning.

Throughout that year, Bren and I went our own separate ways. We weren't talking much or going for walks, but we casually waved to each other from time to time. I was enjoying my relationship with Megan, but I missed Bren's friendship and presence.

In the late Spring of 1993, our sophomore year was coming to a close. I was busy working hard, yet struggling to pay my tuition bills. I was stretched with my study and work schedule. But spiritually, what kept lighting my heart and awakening new fascination of Holy Spirit, are the times when I would read Welsh and Azusa Revival Chronicles. They kept me up late, thinking deeply.

One particular night, I remember laying in my dorm room and reading the words of Frank Bartleman, *"Holy Spirit came in and took over the entire meeting"*...I remember highlighting that and laying the book on my chest and wondering to myself, *"Hmmm...what would that look like?"* Little did I know, that within a matter of just months, I would have a door open to me that would not only answer that question, but also usher me into an encounter with The Holy Spirit that would forever change the course and spiritual trajectory of my life.

A few days later, I had overslept and woke up only to realize that I was late for chapel service. I hurried to brush my teeth and throw on some clothes quickly. As I began to run across campus, it was surprising to see people leaving the chapel service early - with faces filled with anger and frustration. The closer I got to them I could hear them complaining. I was kind of puzzled and very surprised by the number of students who were leaving. I stopped a few of them and asked them, *"Where are you going? Is chapel dismissed? What's wrong?"* Their answers surprised me. They responded, *"Some of our students went over to that silly revival at Carpenters Home Church and they are in there laughing and ruined the meeting...so we're leaving."* I wasn't even aware that anything remotely close to revival was happening in Lakeland at the time...but what made me very curious was why these students were angry. Was it just because other students were *laughing*? I was confused. Were students being laughed at? Were students laughing at a speaker? I had no clue. I kept thinking about my friend, Rusty, whom I knew was the worship pastor there. More students poured out the back of the Chapel, and I stopped them and asked them what was happening...their response was no better...they were angry and said, *"Some of the student body were out of control laughing and causing a commotion in the Chapel...they've been to the revival at Carpenter's*

Home." Sadly, I walked with many of them away from the Chapel. I should have ignored them and their offenses, checking for myself what was happening.

A few days later, I was in my hermeneutics class when suddenly our professor became visibly angry and critical of what had happened in chapel service. He began to warn students not to attend the revival. He said boldly: *"This was a phony revival and that the laughter was nothing more than demons laughing out of the people making a mockery of the word of God! Do not attend this laughing revival!"* Without warning, I was suddenly on my feet with a fire in my spirit bursting forth to our professor, *"Stop! Stop now! You are on the brink of the blasphemy of the Holy Spirit and you must stop now!"* I was in shock! My class was in shock! My professor was in shock! I hadn't been to a single revival meeting at Carpenter's Home Church. As I said, I didn't even know there was anything remotely close to a revival happening in Lakeland, until encountering the angry students that were pouring out of chapel just days before. My professor became very angry with me and told me to sit down and be quiet. Yet again, I implored him: *"No, I will not be quiet. You must stop now and repent for what you are saying…you are on the brink of the blasphemy of the Holy Spirit".* At that point he gave me an option, sit down and be quiet or leave. I chose to leave that class and did not return to sit under that professor again.

I went for a long walk around the campus that afternoon into the early evening. I was so grieved. Friends approached me within hours, as word began to spread around campus about what I had done. I was embarrassed, and yet I knew it was the Spirit of the Lord that had spoken through me. I had little to say to those who questioned me about the class. I was deeply concerned for our professor, and I was grieved by his words and his lack of the fear of The Lord. As with every move of God throughout history, it's grieving beyond words to see critical and opposing voices arise that end up detouring people away from Holy Spirit's wooing.

There was division and territorial aggression. People were divided and opinionated and it made me uncomfortable to say the least. I hadn't even attended the revival, and now people were looking to me and asking why I was defending it, though I had never been. No one came with encouragement for me on the matter, but I knew The Presence of the Lord that quickened me in the classroom, just as I knew His Presence that came upon me in my father's bedroom in 1979.

1 Corinthians 2:14 | NKJV
"But the natural man does not receive the things of the Spirit of God, for they are foolishness to him; nor can he know them, because they are spiritually discerned."

An Invitation & A Divine Set Up

I never made my way over to the revival, as school was quickly wrapping up for the year. Within weeks of arriving back home in Illinois, I received a call from my friend, Rusty. Rusty called and told me that the Carpenter's Home Church was experiencing a significant outpouring of the Spirit and that they were going into their 7th week of meetings. He said, *"Brian it's unexplainable...you just have to experience it!"* He asked me if I would be interested in flying down to play the drums with his worship team for the week (morning and evening services) and just experience what the Lord was doing. Immediately, I responded, *"Yes, I will come! Thank you!"*

The next day I was boarding a plane heading to Tampa not really knowing what to expect, and little did I know that I had a date with destiny – a date that My Father had put on His calendar to meet with me.

When I arrived at the Church that afternoon I can vividly remember walking through the doorway into Heaven's atmosphere. The truth is, every time I recall this memory I get chills and feel the Presence of The Lord. As I walked through the foyer doors of the Church, the tangible fear of the Lord came upon me so powerfully that it nearly took my breath away! I am not exaggerating. I was stunned! Hundreds of people were lying on the ground in the foyer shaking, weeping, moaning, laughing...I was surprised to say the least. Mounds of people were just lost and caught up in His Presence. I felt Holiness. I felt Love and Wonder! There was intensity and fire about the atmosphere...and remember, that was just in the foyer. I had read about this in my studies of The Azusa Revival and the Welsh Revival, but to see it was something completely different!

I carefully stepped over and around the bodies watching people carefully. People were flopping like fish out of water along the bank of a lake...believe me when I say I'm not making light of them...it's what it reminded me of. I will never forget the *sound of their voices.* I was led by one of the church staff down the hall and around back of the stage, where he led me down to the platform. The sanctuary was mammoth – 10,000 seats and packed full of people. But what was more overwhelming than the size of this church was the all-consuming thick and tangible Presence of The King, hanging in the atmosphere! Frank Bartleman's words from 1906 Azusa Outpouring came to mind: *"...my whole being seemed to flow down before Him, like wax before the fire. I lost all consciousness of time and space, being conscious only of His wonderful Presence. I worshiped at His feet. It seemed like a veritable Mount of Transfiguration. I was lost in the pure Spirit. The Lord had nothing for us, but only overwhelmed our spirits by His Presence".*

I had probably the best view in the Church standing up on the stage that afternoon, and I melted like wax in His Presence! And it is true that time fled away at His wonder!

The SOUND...oh, the sound of thousands of people that swept into this blissful romance of the King was overwhelming. Love was in the air and the response was a joy unspeakable and full of glory! Heaven was in that place! His affections were melting my heart. The roar of their laughter was profound. It was both beautiful and scary. I know, that sounds crazy, but it's true. The conviction of The Spirit was pervading the atmosphere. My heart was saying YES, and my mind was saying this is beyond anything I had ever witnessed – not even as a boy or young man, growing up in the Church.

I watched as entire sections of people began to disappear into the floor...falling out of their pews and shaking violently under The Presence, as if someone was in the catwalks as a sniper just taking them out. People were spontaneously getting up, running through the sanctuary and shouting for joy! Others were weeping and moaning from the fire that was falling. Some were singing in heavenly tongues. Children were spinning, dancing and worshipping, caught up in His Presence. For the next hour or more, I stood there under the fear of the Lord with tears pouring down my face watching the dancing hand of God sweep through the people. There was zero hype…zero adrenaline…just raw Jesus!

The minister (who at that time, I knew nothing about, and Rusty never told me his name) quietly walked back and forth across the front of the church, observing what Holy Spirit was doing in the midst of the congregation. He wasn't preaching or teaching. From time to time, he would call someone out of the crowd laying his hand on them and saying, "RIVER" or "FIRE OF GOD"! Each time he did, deep inside me I felt this surging Presence of the Lord in my spirit. I feel it right NOW.

I wept the entire week. I made my way through the worship sets with the team, only to go and find my place of encounter again and again. My eyes were pools and rivers of tears, and my heart was being ignited by His eternal burnings. It was pure Love enveloping and transforming me from the inside. I wept so long and hard it felt like my head had swollen up as big as a pumpkin.

Meeting after meeting, day after day, I sat under the waterfall of Love, and I marveled at His Presence. The sweet new wine of His love escorted me deeper into the chambers of His heart. His wine holds mysterious properties and divine qualities. It satisfies our longings within and unearths the deepest hunger for Him all at once. He lifted me into a place I hadn't been before and opened my eyes to a part of Jesus I hadn't seen before. I've never smoked marijuana, but I can tell you undeniably, I was *high*, more accurately; I was soaring in the high *heavenly places* in Him! I've never been drunk on alcohol, but I can tell you unequivocally, I was "drunk" - Intoxicated by His Love! Just as the Apostle Peter explained on the Day of Pentecost, "*No, this isn't drunkenness; this is the fulfillment of the prophecy of Joel…*" - the pouring out of God's Spirit!

Song of Solomon 1:2 | NASB

"Let him kiss me with the kisses of his mouth – For your love is better than wine."

Psalm 63:3 | NASB

"Because Your loving kindness is better than life, My lips shall praise You."

In the midst of thousands of people I felt like I was sitting alone inside my chrysalis, undergoing a metamorphosis. As the prophet Malachi describes, *"He is like a refiner's fire and a launderer's soap"*. I was being bathed in the fire of His holiness and renouncing every known and unknown sin I had committed that had broken His heart. I have been challenged for more than 20 years to try to adequately describe The Spirit's rush upon his people. It's this beautiful word that we call, *Revival.* Many times, it felt as though we were sitting in a giant wave pool and the Presence of the Lord would roll over us again and again. At other times, I felt like I would burst, not knowing how to handle such a tangible manifest presence of the Lord. The range of human emotion and response to The King's Presence was like shaking champagne bottles up and then popping the corks to spray everywhere!

I witnessed and experienced things that were profound and beyond description. I was washed in a baptism of tears. I felt the love of my Heavenly Father envelope me and consume me. I didn't realize it then, but I can tell you 20+ years later - I was being healed from the inside out – deep, deep, deep in the recesses of my soul. I was being healed by a Love that is not of this world. I could hear Him calling out to me, and all I could do was respond with my simple – YES, LORD!

The altars were packed, as people were being saved and baptized in the Holy Spirit by the hundreds each day. Over 2,200 people were baptized in water that week. Bodies lay all over the Church property under His weighty Presence – in the altars, hallways, bathrooms, parking lot, in the grass, over the hoods of cars. I remember a particular night, at about 1am, helping the ushers carry people out, placing others on dollies, ultimately rolling them to their cars. These folks were beside themselves, experiencing heavenly realities and the joy of our Father. It was beautiful and holy. Anyone who tries to tell you, *laughing revival is shallow water,* frankly doesn't know what he's talking about. For that matter, it wasn't a "laughing revival" – it was Heaven in our midst, and all we could do was respond to His generous access to Love! People always criticize what they don't understand or what they have never tasted experientially. But like the Psalmist said, "*I have tasted and I have seen the Lord is GOOD!*"

Much like the phenomena of the Azusa Outpouring the Lakeland Fire Department came time and again that week as people were calling in to report that the Church building was on fire! Yes, you read that correctly. People were calling in from blocks away and from restaurants down the road saying that the Church was aflame!

During the Azusa Revival, G. H. Lang reports: "*Other eyewitnesses reported seeing a holy glow emanating from the building that could be seen from streets away. Others reported hearing sounds from the wooden building like explosions that reverberated around the neighborhood. Such phenomena caused onlookers to call the Fire Department out on several occasions when a blaze or explosion was reported at the mission building. The Child Welfare Agency tried to shut down the meetings because there were unsupervised children within and around the building at all hours of the day and night. The Health Department tried to stop the meetings because they said the cramped quarters were unsanitary and a danger to public health. God-hungry Christians flocked in from everywhere.*"

As we were nearing the end of that week, I walked off the stage after an amazing worship set. Rusty asked me if I would like to join him and another one of the worship staff to run over to his house to pick up some equipment. I sat in the back of the van and tears began to come once again, as I kept encountering the overwhelming revelation of the holiness of God. I thought to myself, wow, I'm not even on the Church property and it still keeps coming. Sitting in the driveway of Rusty's home, he turned and asked me about what I was feeling. I told him that I have never experienced the depths of God's love like this. Rusty told me that they had prayed before flying me down. They prayed that I would encounter the Lord and feel a heart connection there. Then he surprised me by sharing that they wanted to hire me on their worship staff, and they could find other places for me to serve at the church, so I could build a livable income. Guess what my answer was?

Within a few days I made my way back to Illinois to share with my family, gather my belongings and move back to Lakeland. The Lord was faithful to open additional doors beyond the worship team staff. I served on the housecleaning staff, technical ministry and assisted the junior high ministries. I was vacuuming the 10,000 seat sanctuary, cleaning bathrooms, doors and windows. I was filled with incredible joy serving there at the Church. There was a thick lingering residue of the Presence of the Lord that hung like fog in the sanctuary. During the next 6 months, I took time each day to sit quietly in the sanctuary or lay under a pew and ask the Lord to use my life. I was overcome with a longing for significance and purpose.

Megan and I were engaged that Summer. Bren had been serving in Zimbabwe, Africa on a missions outreach. I hadn't seen her for quite awhile. One night, during the Fall, while visiting Megan at Southeastern, I saw Bren from a distance walking across the parking lot near the women's dorms. I told Megan I wanted to take a minute to go and say hello to her and ask her about missions adventure. I walked down the parking lot to where Bren was visiting a friend, and we began catching up on life. While she was talking and sharing some stories, suddenly the conviction of the Holy Spirit took me by storm - so thick. I was feeling uncomfortable and was wondering to myself, "*Wow, what's going on here?*" I was starting to feel convicted about my engagement to Megan. At that moment, I heard the Holy Spirit whisper to me, "*You know you're not supposed to be engaged to her, because you're going to marry Bren!*" I was stunned! My heart was pounding! I started arguing with The Lord in my mind about Bren. After all, being with John throughout these years. And, I had made my commitment to Megan. It was then that I made a conscious decision to not tell Bren that I had gotten engaged. I thought I would just wrap up the conversation as quickly as I could and walk away.

To my surprise, Bren then said to me, *"So, I hear you got engaged."* It was like she kicked me in the stomach. I didn't know what to say. She just stared at me. She did not congratulate me or say anything sweet or encouraging...she just stared at me. I can only imagine what my face looked like. I responded, *"Yes."* I was so utterly uncomfortable that I wrapped up the conversation as quickly as possible and walked away. It was unsettling to say the least.

I went back to my apartment that night confused, embarrassed and feeling very unsure about my future. I never told Megan. I knew that I loved her, and that I had made a commitment to her and her family. I was convinced that Bren and John would end up getting married. Hadn't they dated on and off for the last several years? Nothing made any sense. I knew I heard the voice of the Lord that night, but I didn't know how to respond.

Consecration & Blast Off!

In January of 1994, Rodney Howard-Browne returned to Carpenters Home for "Camp Meeting". LOVE CAME DOWN! Once again, tens of thousands packed the Church campus to encounter The Holy Spirit. If I had a time-traveling DeLorean with a flux capacitor, I'd crank that baby up to 88 miles an hour and take you there! It was God's tangible glory and fire!

It was the second week during a morning session that The Lord began to speak to me. I had just finished worship time with the band and found my seat in the sanctuary. While Rodney was teaching, my mind was traveling back to places I had read about in college with The Azusa and Welsh Revival. He began to remind me of prayers I had prayed on the college campus, and then he showed me I was going to be leaving Carpenter's Home Church to serve Rodney. Whoa! That was not on my radar! That night, I walked the aisle to the altar and made a fresh consecration of my life unto The Lord. Long before Brian and Jenn Johnson (Bethel Music) would pen the words to the beautiful song – *"Where You go, I'll go and what You say, I'll say"*...I laid down at the altar and wept before the Lord and prayed earnestly, *that I would go where he told me to go, I would be who He desired me to be, I would say what He desires me to say...I promised The Lord that my heart was fully His, and He could do what He wished to do in my life.* One additional and very significant thing I did that night was I laid my relationship and engagement on the altar before The Lord. I told The Lord that if our relationship was not ordained of Him, then I gave Him permission to take Megan out of my life. I repented for going my own way and not yielding my dreams for a spouse fully unto Him. It scared me to pray that prayer, because I had already promised her my future, but I wanted God's will more than anything else. Just as God answered David's prayer and sacrifice by sending fire from heaven, God would answer that prayer with the fire of His love in the coming months.

Three days later after a morning session I was relaxing in my apartment with my two roommates, as we had to get back to the church for the evening meeting. The phone rang, and to my surprise, it was Rodney! At first I thought it was one of my buddies trying to talk like him with his South African dialect...and I laughed and said, "*Who is this?*" He said, "*It's Rodney.*" I said, "*Yeah, yeah, ok, who is this?*" He said, "*It's Rodney.*" He started to laugh at me, and then I realized it was really him (no one laughs like Rodney), and I got nervous. He invited me to come over to the home where he was staying for the Camp Meeting, so he could talk with me. I dressed up quickly in a suit and tie, and when I arrived, I found Rodney, all his family, and his staff in shorts, just chilling and swimming in the pool. Boy did I feel out of place.

His wife told me he was on the phone with Kenneth Copeland, and that he would be with me in a few moments. She gave me a hot tea, and as I waited in the living room, I was thinking about what the Lord had told me days before – about leaving the Church to serve Rodney. As Rodney sat down he asked me how I was enjoying the meetings. We had a great talk about the moving of the Spirit, the worship and so on and so forth...He was very hospitable. He asked me if God was saying anything to me. I was nervous not knowing how to answer that, and I surely didn't want to just come out and tell him that the Lord had told me I was going to serve him. I was young, dumb and a little cocky, so I said to him, *"If God wants you to know what He saying to me, He'll tell you."* He started laughing at me. Then he said, *"Well ok, if God told you that you are going to come with me on the road, you should go ahead and tell me now."* I was surprised. I said, *"Yes, He did."* Rodney said that the Lord had told him about a week ago, and he shared that he had already talked to my Pastor, my friends, coworkers and the treasurer to see if I tithed and was a giver. I was impressed; this guy wasn't messing around! He offered me a position to come with him and serve as his assistant to help his family, be his drummer for his worship team on the road and help him with any needs that would arise. Guess what my answer was?

The next 9 months of 1994 traveling with Rodney was a special gift from My Heavenly Father! I could write a book on just the experiences and encounters I had and witnessed firsthand throughout our Nation, seeing the harvest and the wonders of God! Jesus enlarged my world, my heart, my faith and understanding experientially! Not only was my world revolutionized, 1994 was a year that changed and challenged the spiritual landscape of the Church at large in renewal and revival. It was a forerunning year, breaking us into victories we are living in right now. My friend, Randy Clark, was used as a catalyst that year in Toronto, and another great geyser of His Presence was released to the Nations! Fires were igniting and spreading everywhere. I saw and met many of the Generals that are being used in the earth today to shake nations, and I met them when no one knew their names. I saw them on floors of auditoriums and gathering across the country drunk in the Spirit encountering their First Love, and now their ministries are carriers of this fire and books are circulated throughout the world about the fruit that came forth from the touch of God! Though it would take me an extra year to complete my bible college training, serving Rodney was one of the greatest privileges The Lord ever gave me as a young man, and I honor him and his wife Adonica (and their precious family) as God's Pioneers! I'm forever grateful that they obeyed The Lord's call and commission so many years ago to leave South Africa and come to their *mission field* called America!

There is one particular experience that I feel will help give context to where the Holy Spirit is leading me for the later portions of the book. It happened in Washington DC. In February 1994, we were in a crusade at a large church. Rodney had called the staff together and shared the news that he was asked to speak at The Pentagon. Yes, I know...WOW! I will never forget that cold snowy winter morning driving over to the Pentagon and walking through the door and down the hallways. My spirit was at attention, and I felt a shift coming in the atmosphere. The auditorium was prepared for hundreds of military dignitaries and governmental officials. I was sitting off to the side of the stage as Rodney took the podium. His message that morning was, *God Loves America*. It was powerful and rich with anointing. He didn't thunder his message. He brought it with tremendous sensitivity and humility. I watched the audience as they were visibly moved and affected by the Presence of The Lord, as Rodney shared God's great affection for our people, our hope and destiny. I can't fully explain what happened to me, but a mantle for our Nation came upon my life that morning. God opened my spirit and let me see and hear the cry coming up out of my generation and those yet to come. Intercession burst and was set aflame in my spirit. He reminded me of my dream in Junior High School soaring over the four corners of our nation as a mighty eagle. I saw National Awakening – in the streets, colleges and business sector – I saw transformed cities. I saw a holy raging fire burning in the youth of America...it was unbridled passion for Jesus that looked nothing like "Church". I was changed that day. And it's never lifted off of me.

The Voice of God

In June, God moved in my life in a very swift and peculiar way. My engagement was suddenly over; Megan broke off the relationship as we were going in different directions. I knew it was Lord, but it hurt so deeply! Thankfully, Rodney and other seasoned men of God strengthened and encouraged my heart in those days – helping to keep me focused on God's divine purposes.

On July 7th, I was in Louisville, Kentucky preparing for the summer camp meeting and working in the ministry headquarters. One of the secretaries from the front office came back and said they had a message for me. She handed me a piece of paper with a name on it and a phone number from Columbus, Ohio. I didn't know anyone from Columbus. I kept looking at the name, but couldn't figure out who it was as the secretary had written the name down incorrectly. While dialing the numbers, I suddenly realized, "*Oh, Dear Jesus, – This is BREN!*" A gentle beautiful voice came on the end of the line and sure enough – it was her! I was shaking and trembling and wondering why she called the ministry office? How did she know where I was? How did she even know I was working for Rodney's ministry? How did she get the number? The moment, I heard Bren's voice I could see myself in my mind's eye standing before her there on the college campus and hearing The Lord say, "*You know you're not supposed to be engaged to Megan, because you're going to marry Bren!*" God had my attention!

Bren shared that she had been praying for me a lot. She noted how The Holy Spirit kept bringing me up before her in prayer, and she couldn't relent. She indicated that she kept thinking about our friendship and wondered where I was. She wanted to know if I had gotten married, so I told her that the engagement and the relationship was over, and I explained the details to her. We talked for maybe 30 minutes that afternoon. She told me that she was thankful to hear that I hadn't gotten married, as she felt in her spirit that it wasn't right. She also told me that her relationship with John was over and that she would like me to come visit her sometime in Columbus. Hmmm...where do think I went after camp meeting? Yep, you guessed it...Columbus.

Rodney gave me a week off, as I told him about Bren's call and how I wanted to go and see her and my family in Illinois. As I drove from Louisville to Columbus, I kept wondering if the Lord had spoken to Bren. Did He show her we were going to be together? I couldn't wait to see her. I was overjoyed with thanksgiving and the awareness of God's goodness and grace over my life – once again realigning my path with Bren.

The days in Columbus were so special. Bren and I went for long walks just as we had in college - reconnecting and catching up on life. I shared with her what I had been encountering with The Lord in the past year. There are no words to describe how

I felt being with her, knowing that both of our old relationships were now removed and wondering what was about to unfold.

My last day in Columbus, before heading to Illinois to see my family, was quite interesting. Bren and I went out for lunch and over to a park where she told me that she had something important to tell me. I thought that she was going to tell me that she was in love with me and that we were meant to be together. I was ready to tell her what the Lord had told me on the college campus that night when she returned from Africa. To my surprise, Bren said, *"I like you, I really like you, I cherish our friendship, but I want you to know that we are just friends...like in college...nothing more, just friends."* I gathered my manly confidence and responded, *"Oh yeah, I know that."* Truthfully, at that moment, I was imploding on the inside.

Later that afternoon, I left for Illinois, and I cried most of the way there not understanding what was happening in my life. I was so disappointed in myself. The puzzle pieces were not fitting together, and I was desperate to understand His working in my life. God had swiftly removed my engagement. Lovingly, Bren was moved by His Spirit to pray earnestly for me and find me - and now, Bren wants me to know that we are just *friends*. Wow! I was broken...but God was working all things together for our good.

I spent a few days home with my family resting and trying to make sense of the journey. One afternoon, a Pastor who had been friends with my Mom and Dad for years called the house and asked my Dad if I would be interested in coming over to their church to share what I had been experiencing and seeing on the road with Rodney. I was in no place emotionally to go and share the goodness of God, but the Pastor was pretty persuasive, so I reluctantly said that I would come. I didn't know it, but God was setting me up for a massive breakthrough and a significant prophetic impartation!

The service that morning turned out to be a beautiful meeting, rich with The Presence of The Lord. After everyone had left the building, the Pastor's wife told my Dad that she had a prophetic word for me and asked if she could share it.

She turned to me with eyes like fire! I suddenly felt God's Presence rush upon me. She pointed her finger at me and with bold authority announced, *"YOU ARE AN EAGLE! YOU ARE AN EAGLE! YOU ARE AN EAGLE! And the wind of the Spirit of God is going to blow into your wings and carry you high above this storm that you are facing, and He is going to take you into the heavenly places and transform you. He is going to blow you to the four corners of this Nation with the burning fire of His Presence! You will light His fire everywhere you go! The Lord also says that He is preparing your wife for you even now! This will be a very quick work! So quick, that the next time that she sees you and lays eyes upon you, she will know that you are her husband!"*

I was shaking on the inside and the outside under a weightiness of God's Presence! I was stunned by this word! Absolutely stunned! But I was also empowered, as it filled me with hope! My mind was overcome with imagery from the dreams I had dreamt long ago in Jr. and Senior High - soaring as a mighty eagle over America. I was baffled because I had told no one of this dream, nor did I understand what it meant all those years ago. But that day, God lovingly revealed my purpose and destiny to be His messenger of fire. When I heard the word about my *wife being prepared quickly,* I was in awe because I was scheduled to meet back up with the revival team in Dallas, Texas and guess who was planning to come to the crusade with her sister? Yep, you guessed it! BREN!

Four days later, we met back up. True to His word, at an altar in Rockwall, Texas, The Lord spoke to Bren that I was her husband! We courted for one year and were married August 19th, 1995 in Columbus, Ohio.

Special Note: I have taken some time to share some of our story, because Bren and I know how vitally important it is for those praying and seeking a spouse to follow the voice of The Lord at all cost. Our story was not perfect, but God who is perfect made all things work together for our good. And what he has done for us, he can do for you. He is faithful, and He can cause everything to shift in your favor when we humble ourselves and seek him wholeheartedly. One of the greatest decisions you will ever make is the one in which you decide whom to marry – the one to whom you will devote the rest of your life. Bren and I release our faith and pray for those who are seeking and believing for a spouse right now, that your destiny will converge with the one whom God has chosen and ordained for your faith journey and life adventure!

CHAPTER TWO

THE BURNING ONE

O ur God is an all-consuming fire. The Scriptures tell us that everything around God is ablaze because of the fire of His holiness. The Prophet Daniel describes His Mighty Throne ablaze: *"I watched as thrones were put in place and the Ancient One sat down to judge. His clothing was as white as snow, his hair like purest wool.* **He sat on a fiery throne with wheels of blazing fire,** *and* **a river of fire was pouring out, flowing from his presence.** *Millions of angels ministered to him; many millions stood to attend him..."* (Daniel 7:9&10 NLT)

The Apostle John in the book of Revelation spoke of The Burning One and wrote: **"...and in the midst of the seven lampstands One like** *the Son of Man, clothed with a garment down to the feet and girded about the chest with a golden band. His head and hair were white like wool, as white as snow,* **and His eyes like a flame of fire; His feet were like fine brass, as if refined in a furnace,** *and His voice as the sound of many waters; He had in His right hand seven stars, out of His mouth went a sharp two-edged sword, and* **His countenance was like the sun shining in its strength."** (Revelation 1:13-16 NKJV)

When the prophet Ezekiel encountered the throne of God, he

beheld The Burning One and wrote: *"Above this surface was something that looked like a throne made of blue lapis lazuli. And on this throne high above was **a figure whose appearance resembled a man. From what appeared to be his waist up, he looked like gleaming amber, flickering like a fire. And from his waist down, he looked like a burning flame, shining with splendor.** All around him was a glowing halo, like a rainbow shining in the clouds on a rainy day. This is what the glory of the Lord looked like to me. When I saw it, I fell face down on the ground..."* (Ezekiel 1:26-28 NLT)

Seraphim are the angels who worship all around the burning throne of Almighty God. The word seraphim means, *"burning ones".* The prophet Isaiah described these fiery heavenly angels as ones who have six wings and worship above the Lord on His throne. (Isaiah 6:1&2)

To encounter God is to encounter fire – His burning, holy unquenchable love! The Holy Spirit is known as "the Spirit of burning." The Holy Spirit manifests before the throne as seven flaming lamps of fire – seven for perfection, completeness and wisdom. *"And from the throne proceeded lightnings, thunderings, and voices. Seven lamps of fire were burning before the throne, which are the seven Spirits of God.* (Revelation 4:5 NASB)

In 1997, Bren and I launched Light The Fire Ministries in obedience to the call of God and the burden of The Lord. We had been ministering on staff for three years serving in a local charismatic church outside of Columbus, Ohio, but our hearts were burning for national revival. By faith, we stepped out and God lovingly met us, enveloping us in a grace much larger than we could ever have anticipated. Our first extended revival meeting went six weeks, which was a massive stretch for a 24-year-old revivalist armed with 5 burning messages from the Lord, one of them a message I had *borrowed* from Pastor John Kilpatrick of the Brownsville Revival. The Lord met us in a remarkable way, refreshing the church, as I was learning how to receive a fresh word from Him daily – a word to pour out to hungry hearts.

By September of 1998, our ministry was gaining favorable momentum and thankfully my message portfolio was increasing as well. But everything was about to change as we visited a Church in Central Illinois. We didn't know it, but God had marked His calendar to meet us in the most spectacular way!

We were scheduled to be in meetings Sunday morning through Wednesday night. The church family had been faithfully praying for about two years for the Lord to move in their midst. Something electric and tangible was in the air the very first morning, as the church was packed with hungry souls. It is no exaggeration to say that the fire of His Holiness descended upon us that day. Love came down and there was a notable release of power – far surpassing anything we had been seeing. We extended the meetings for another week, as people were coming to be saved and delivered. A few weeks spilled over into a few months, as a notable outpouring of God's Presence enveloped us. People were drawn from an 8 State radius as word spread of the open heavens that had invaded Springfield, Illinois. The revival became a rallying point for thousands to encounter God's manifest presence.

By January 1999, I had preached over 100 times in the Springfield Revival since that first September morning. God had yoked us to His unrelenting plow for the spiritual field of the Midwest. Bren's birthday was coming and she had made plans to get away to Florida with some intercessor friends for a Morning Star Conference. As Bren and the ladies went south to Florida, I made my way back from Cincinnati to Illinois to continue in our meetings. Bren's sister had given me a *tape* (you remember those, right? Tapes are these little plastic boxes with turning wheels...) by a revivalist named Tommy Tenney, who had just released a new book called *The God Chasers*. Up until that day I had never heard of Tommy (He's become a dear friend to us over the years). The tape was not powerful preaching, but rather, a broken man weeping his way through a message about encountering the glory of God. The more he shared, the more I wept. His desperation and brokenness resounded with the deep cry of my heart for more of God! The Presence of the Lord was so thick in my car that I wept and trembled for five hours, as I made my way back to the Church in Springfield.

J E S U S – The Burning Man!

When I finally arrived, I was still under the heavy weight of the Lord's Presence - my body and hands were noticeably trembling. Though I was burning, I summoned the courage to ask for MORE. I was so hungry to be consumed by God. I made a plan to sneak into the side entry of the Church without being seen by any staff or intercessors. Frankly, I didn't want this beautiful experience I was having with The Holy Spirit to lift off of me.

As I made my way into the building, I cut through the Sanctuary and headed over to the older part of the campus where we had an office. My steps got heavier and slower, and my eyelids became heavy. I felt like I was walking through waste deep waters with strong currents. As I made my way slowly through the dimly lit Sanctuary and up the stairs towards my office, it felt like I passed through a veil or a thick curtain on my face. As I did, I collapsed against the wall and began to tremble on the floor. I started to get scared, as God's Presence was increasing. After what may have been 10 minute on the floor, I shimmied up the wall to gain my balance and walked slowly about another ten feet only to walk through another invisible veil and collapse once more. This time, the trembling was increasing all over my body and the fear of the Lord was so strong I felt like I would burst. Again, I made it to my feet after another 10 minutes on the floor and finally made it into my private office. I shut the door behind me, dropped my bag down on the couch and fell into the chair weeping.

Deafening silence filled the room. Though I was trembling, I was sober and my spirit was at full attention. I became fearfully aware of the Presence of Jesus. Yes, Jesus! It was different than The Holy Spirit…perhaps it's not different at all, but my spirit was aware that Jesus was present. I don't know how to theologically unpack that as I understand The Father, Son and Holy Spirit are One and in perfect union. But this was different and I knew The Lord was very near and present. As if I had earphones on my head, I began to hear His sandals brushing across the carpet coming slowly down the hallway and the terror of the Lord overcame me. I cried out, *"Lord, I'm not ready for this!"* The Burning

One appeared in the office with penetrating all consuming force. His Presence was overwhelming, all enveloping and permeating every pore of my body like a fire. The force that emanated from Him had the sensation of tiny rivulets of sand coursing through my entire body. Unexplainable power was sweeping through my face, chest, stomach, back and legs. The currents felt as though they were passing straight through me, and like a mighty vacuum His presence was returning back to Himself – pulling, eradicating and extracting a darkness out of me that I had never known to be present within. I closed my eyes and gasped at His Presence. It was beautiful, terrifying and powerful. I absorbed His loving essence. I felt weightless as if submerged under water. The silence was amplified in my ears. It's hard to find the words to describe this...but then suddenly, He was gone.

I opened my eyes and sat in the chair for more than an hour with intense burnings and shaking. The weightiness started to lift and it once again became bearable for me to move. I could finally move my legs and was able to lay down on the floor as electric waves coursed through me. I kept seeing this piercing vision of the Lord anointing me with His blood. I was bowed down kneeling before him and His hand was upon my forehead. From His hand, was a stream of His blood flowing down over my head and fully covering me. I started wondering if I had just experienced an open vision or a theophany (the appearance of The Lord). You may think it's ridiculous to ask such a thing, but you must understand that this was so supernatural and far beyond any encounter with God that I had ever known. Nothing in all my life had ever happened like this. I wondered to myself why He didn't say a word...But in His Presence, I was fully apprehended and turned into another man!

A few hours later, I freshened up, walked out of the office and headed into the intercessory prayer room. I found it filled with passionate prayer warriors, preparing for the night's service. I remained quiet, and never saying a word about the visitation. (In fact, until this book, I've only shared this encounter with my wife, my children, and a few close friends and have only publically spoken of the encounter 3 times in the last 14+ years. It is deeply holy to me.)

The meeting began as people packed into the Sanctuary. Worship was strong and the place was filled with praise, hunger and expectation. After about an hour of worship I was welcomed to the platform to bring the word. As I stepped behind the pulpit it felt like my ears were plugged up with water, and I felt like I was once again submerged deep within the ocean of His Presence. I had a keen awareness of His nearness once again. I was trying to greet the people, but I started to get fearful that the Lord was going to walk into the Sanctuary. I silenced myself as I tried to figure out what to do. To my surprise, people spontaneously began to weep and moan openly throughout the congregation. The atmosphere shifted quickly, as the Sanctuary was filled with bursting emotions of joy and weeping. The King's Presence filled the house! I slid down behind the pulpit and laid there all night, as The Holy Spirit had His way with the people. For the next 4 months of revival, we sunk into the bottomless depths of His oceans of Love. It was glorious! People were transformed, healed and made whole in His Presence. Sickness and diseases were eradicated. Bodies were made whole. Barren women were given children. Hundreds were baptized in fire. Ministers were ignited afresh and began exporting flaming coals of revival back to their regions. Angels came on assignment with gifts and ministry. People were caught up into heaven during the meetings with visions and encounters with the Lord. It was beautiful...it was holy...it was pure revival!

Pursue An Encounter

"I want the presence of God Himself, or I don't want anything at all to do with religion... I want all that God has or I don't want any."
A.W Tozer

I believe is it vitally important for every believer to hunger and seek a greater encounter with The Lord. It is normal for a believer to long and desire to know God more intimately. Nothing has fueled my hunger for the more of God than reading His Word and spending quality time with The Holy Spirit in prayer. The Apostle Paul wrote, *"Yes, everything else is worthless when compared with the infinite value of knowing Christ Jesus my Lord."* (Philippians 3:8 NLT) I believe you are hungry for more of God, and you desire to experience His Presence in tangible ways. As you read through this book, I pray that it will be fuel for your heart to pursue God's face, and that you begin to encounter His holiness and burnings. Perhaps, even more importantly, I desire that you become aware that God is actively pursuing you for the sole purpose of *encounter* – to know you and make Himself known to you! It is through encounter with God that He reveals that we belong fully unto Him – our Father and Creator. Nothing delivers one's soul from an orphan spirit more powerfully than an encounter with God. His intention is to love you unconditionally and fill your heart with the beauty of His holiness. Most good relationships are built from many encounters over a long period of time. And, though God is incomprehensibly big and full of mystery, He desires to make Himself known to you.

The word *encounter* conveys the idea of an unforeseen meeting. When Peter, James and John walked up on the mountain with the Lord, they never could have imagined that Jesus would be transfigured before their very eyes and His heavenly glory would be manifested for them to behold. They had no idea that something life changing was about to happen. Suddenly, The Lord was turned inside out with a dazzling display of His glory. This encounter was so remarkable that even Moses and Elijah showed up as well. (Matthew 17) I think it's very notable that Jesus told them not to tell of this encounter they had witnessed until an appointed time. I believe many things that God reveals to us privately are not always open for public consumption and that our stewardship of holy things is a sure test. Divine encounters are initiated by God. They cannot be manufactured. Divine encounters are available for those who hunger and desire to know God. We must seek first The King and His kingdom. Jesus promised, *"Blessed are the pure in heart, for they shall see God."* The Bible accounts describe God having unexpected and life changing interactions with people. Since the Lord never changes, He continues to deal with humanity in powerful, unanticipated ways.

An encounter with God can happen anywhere—at home, in church, on a walk, or while driving—but what is certain, wherever He shows up, you will always feel an awesome sense of His loving presence and holiness. When Isaiah went to the temple one day, he had no idea that something life changing was about to happen. Isaiah encountered *"...the Lord sitting on a throne, high and lifted up, with the train of His robe filling the temple."* (Isaiah 6) When the Lord appeared to Isaiah, He was accompanied by angelic beings who covered their faces in utter reverence for His absolute purity and perfection as they cried out, *"Holy, holy, holy, is the Lord of hosts."* This glimpse into the spiritual dimension overwhelmed Isaiah with an awareness of God's glory and holiness. We cannot be so bound to virtual reality in this life that it keeps us from truly apprehending His nearness in the unseen realm. His kingdom is at hand and His name is still *Immanuel* – which means, *God with us.*

Hunger That Transforms

"Every move of God can be traced back to a kneeling figure."
Revivalist, D.L. Moody

In the mid 90's, after the Salvadoran Civil War, Bren and I were ministering in the jungles of El Salvador. Our missionary host had brought us to a church (a small shack) in the mountainous region to lodge. Our team's stay would prove to be quite adventurous, as the church was filled with special guests each night – huge tarantula spiders, hungry mosquitoes and vampire bats. I'm not kidding!

The day we arrived, our host shared a remarkable story with us. Apparently, where we were camping was a historical landmark that had become a rallying point for the Presence of God. The church was known as the *Azusa of Central America*. Miraculously, in 1907, the Pastor had received word of the Azusa outpouring of the Holy Spirit in Los Angeles. He was desperately hungry for more of God and seeking the baptism of fire. His burden and vision for El Salvador was overwhelming. He had tarried many years, desiring to be baptized with the Holy Spirit. Upon hearing word of what God was doing in Los Angeles, the pastor set out courageously taking a boat up the west coast of Central America and Mexico all the way to southern California. That's courageous hunger!

Finally, arriving under the open heavens of LA, the pastor was gloriously baptized in the Holy Spirit's fire and was transformed into another man! He stayed for weeks, receiving teaching and impartation from William Seymour and Frank Bartleman, after which he made the journey back to El Salvador.

After months on the sea, this man on fire returned to his homeland with heaven's treasure, and *Pentecost* hit Central America! It's remarkable what one man's burning and unrelenting hunger was able to impart. One man prepared the way for future generations.

That night, long after the team went to bed, I stayed up praying at the altar, (safely nestled under my mosquito net watching the bats of course) riveted by the story of this man's hunger and utter desperation for more of God. His hunger prepared the way for more than he could have ever imagined. His baptism became the torch to Nations. Let's be honest. Most of us would never even contemplate making a sacrifice like that. But, then he actually made the journey to LA, of all places! Whoever this man was, his hunger and passion were colossal! I humbly cried out to the Lord to possess me with the same unquenchable hunger and burning appetite that this pioneer carried!

Spiritual Cravings & Longings

Hunger means PASSION for GOD! Our spiritual cravings and longings for God are what will determine the direction of our lives. Hunger determines destiny. Ever had a craving? Sure you have! You know just what I'm talking about! It's 11pm and you know you shouldn't eat late, yet you start craving a fully loaded supreme pizza with extra cheese...Oh, yes! Or you have those wild ones you dare not share with your friends...for me; it's normally a Dairy Queen heath blizzard for breakfast! Call it crazy, but I hate to admit how often I crave them...thankfully I have that one pretty subdued!

> *Jesus said,* **"Blessed are those who hunger and thirst for righteousness, For they shall be filled."**
> Matthew 5:6 | NKJV

Do you crave God? Do you hunger for His friendship daily? I have come to know experientially that it's only His Presence that truly satisfies the hunger and deepest longings of my soul. Craving deeper friendship with God has become the greatest adventure of my life.

Hunger for more of God's manifest glory should be the norm for a follower of Jesus. It's not something unusual - reserved for only a few impassioned pioneers. The normal state of a Christian is to be thirsty and hungry for God. In the natural we eat and are satisfied, but in the kingdom the more we *taste and see that the Lord is good*, the hungrier we become. (Ps 34:8) Hunger for God is the place of absolute dependency on the Lord. The more we experience His Love and riches, the more our spirit yearns to encounter His glory. The Bible tells us that God, "*satisfies the thirsty and fills the hungry with good things*" (Ps. 107:9).

David, the passionate psalmist recognized and discerned these deep inner longings of the heart and yearnings for the Presence of God. Many times throughout the Psalms, we find him meditating, offering worship and praise, or crying out to God. His greatest joy was to be with his heavenly Father in intimate communion.

> *"O God, You are my God; Early will I seek You; My soul thirsts for You; My flesh longs for You In a dry and thirsty land, Where there is no water."*
> Psalm 63:1 | NET

> *"How lovely are Your dwelling places, O LORD of hosts. My soul longs, yes, even faints For the courts of the LORD; My heart and my flesh cry out for the living God."*
> Psalm 84:1-2 | NIV

I think it's important to note that if our soul and flesh can hunger for more of God, this reveals that our soul and flesh can also be completely and wholly satisfied by Him! With God, it is no contradiction that within the same heart you can be completely fulfilled in Him and yet awakened deeply with new cravings of the soul by His wooing.

> *"For He satisfies the longing soul, And fills the hungry soul with goodness."*
> Psalm 107:9 | NLT

Unbridled cravings and desires that burn for anything other than God can be dangerous. The capacity within our hearts for true satisfaction can only be found in the One who is bottomless and limitless Love! He is to be our magnificent obsession. To taste of His perfection and holiness will capture a life completely. Jesus specifically revealed that our burning obsession must only be God..."*You shall love the Lord your God with ALL your heart, with ALL your soul, and with ALL your mind.*" (Matthew 22:37) This is total abandonment – you must be ALL in! Not casual but consumed! It is hunger that keeps us in the pursuit of Him!

> *"It is the glory of God to conceal a matter, But the glory of kings is to search out a matter."*
> Proverbs 25:2 | NKJV

Many years ago I had a dream that I was out on the ocean with some of the great and notable spiritual generals and revivalists of our day. Some of them happen to be personal friends. As we were preparing our diving equipment, excitement filled the boat, anticipating the day's discovery. I was overjoyed and thankful just to be a part of this dive with such great leaders. As I was cleaning my mask, I remember Tommy Tenney smiling at me and saying, "You ready?" We dove off the side of the boat and began to swim deeper together as a team. I got to a certain place in the dive and became aware that I was experiencing shortness of breath, realizing I needed to return to the boat. I was disappointed, as I watched the others diving deeper to explore the coral reef. I waited for their return. When they gathered back into the boat, sharing the beauty of the reef, filled with a vast array of colorful fish, I became jealous. We dove a second time and I had the same experience. Once again, gathered in the boat, they shared the beauty of the depths. My longings and frustrations were increasing. Finally, on the third dive, my experience was no different.

Then the Lord took me above the boat to see the team from a higher vantage point. To my surprise, I became aware that everyone was wearing scuba gear, but I was wearing snorkeling gear. This made it impossible for me to go exploring the depths I so longed to reach.

I woke up and heard the Lord clearly, "*Son you have longed to swim in the depths of my heart discovering my riches, and today I'm going to give you a gear upgrade that you may discover me freely with no restrictions."*

Gear Upgrades for Encounter

Are you in need of a gear upgrade? Are you aware that there are deeper Waters to swim and explore? The Holy Spirit can take you there. He's the guide into Father's bottomless depths of Love and Glory! Just as Jesus used parables to conceal truth for those who were truly hungry, so it is that the Holy Spirit invites us on a quest to discover The God who has hidden Himself for us to find. Again, *"It is the glory of God to conceal a matter, But the glory of kings is to search out a matter."* The quest of hungry and passionate souls is the *deep calling unto deep.* I'm sending you a personal invitation to go deep sea dive the unfathomable depths of His heart! I invite you to pursue the face of God with burning zeal to encounter His glory and wonder, that you may be transformed into another man - into the burning image of the Son of Man!

We can learn something from William Seymour, of the great Azusa Outpouring, whose hunger for God was unquenchable! William hungered for the baptism of the Spirit with a fire so deep that he was praying five hours a day. And, if that wasn't enough, he "upgraded" to seven. He earnestly prayed that he would receive this baptism of fire that Charles Parham had preached about. John G. Lake tells the story of William Seymour that: *"God had put such a hunger into that man's heart that when the fire of God came it glorified him. I do not believe any other man in modern times had a more wonderful deluge of God in his life than what God gave that dear fellow, and the glory and power of a real Pentecost swept the world."*

William Seymour was a man on fire - a man possessed by the Spirit of God to father revival on the planet in his day! May God glorify this generation with his baptism of fire and glory to set the world on fire! The Apostle Peter said on the day of Pentecost that the promise of The Holy Spirit was to "every generation"."*Then Peter said to them, "Repent, and let every one of you be baptized in the name of Jesus Christ for the remission of sins; and **you shall receive the gift of the Holy Spirit.***

*For the promise is to you and to your children, and
to all who are afar off, as many as the Lord our
God will call."*
Acts 2:38&29 | NKJV

Stewarding The Fire!

*"Let a man so consider us, as servants of Christ and stewards of
the mysteries of God. Moreover it is required in stewards
that one be found faithful."*
1 Corinthians 4:1&2 | NKJV

Stewardship is a paramount principle in the kingdom. The Apostle Paul called himself a *"steward of the mysteries of God."* You and I are called to faithfully steward the mysteries of the Kingdom. One of the greatest mysteries is how God comes and causes the human heart to burn with holy passion and zeal for Him! We must guard the flame with the holy jealousy that rests within our heart - allowing absolutely nothing to extinguish it!

Guarding your heart is your personal responsibility - good stewardship. (Proverbs 4:23) If you desire to be consumed by your *"First Love"*, you must train your heart to be hungry for His holiness. We need an appetite that can only be satisfied by God alone! If we're going to steward a burning heart we must have an insatiable appetite and desire for the manifest presence of God!

*"In His presence is fullness of joy and at his right hand are
pleasures forevermore."*
Psalm 16:11 | ESV

I'm desperately hungry for the fullness of joy and holy ecstasy that comes from being in the manifest Presence of God! I'm hungry to drink from the river of his pleasure and ultimately I'm thirsty for nearness. I want God more than anything else that is made available to me. I want more than just peace. I want His Presence! A foundational key to developing and cultivating the Presence of God in your life is discovered in spending time with God in the secret place.

Leonard Ravenhill is quoted saying, *"that the secret to prayer is praying in secret."* I know I can be *God conscious* throughout the course of my day, and I can *practice the presence of God* anywhere and anytime, but there is something that happens when I begin to find myself *alone* with the Holy Spirit on a consistent basis. It's called intimacy. Intimacy is found as we synchronize our heartbeat with that of God. It's why Jesus tells us in Matthew 5 to pray in secret, because *"our Father who is in the secret place will reward you..."* I love corporate worship and the corporate prayer room setting, but neither one should take the place of meeting with God alone. In fact, it is only when we consistently find ourselves with the Lord in secret, that we then begin to permeate the fragrance of His anointing and ultimately begin to host the manifest presence of God.

> *"You who seek God, your hearts shall live."*
> Psalm 69:32 | ASV

When we begin to seek God and spend time soaking in His presence in secret, our hearts cannot help but burn! We become fully alive on the inside! When this becomes the reality of our lives, we cause other hearts to burn with desire for God and His glory!

Remember the story of the men walking with the Lord, the Burning One, to Emmaus? When two men encountered Jesus on the road to Emmaus, they said that their *"hearts were burning"* while He spoke with them (Luke 24:32). In my life, the men and women that have impacted me the most are the ones who when they open their mouth to speak, set my heart on fire and provoke me to "holy jealousy"! Every one of these individuals is a person who places the highest premium on living in the secret place - giving him or herself over to spending time in God's presence daily!

By developing an appetite for God's presence, we will not only continue to steward a burning heart, but we will also become agents of revival and awakening which may cause other hearts to burn with passion for Jesus. It's time we begin to ask God to make us hungry for His presence again. What I have learned in my grand adventure with God is that, if we ask, He'll respond generously!

Created to Burn

Romans 12:11 | AMP
"Never lag in zeal and in earnest endeavor; be aglow and burning with the Spirit, serving the Lord."

You and I were created to burn for God! Our assignment on the earth is to be a burning and shining lamp which stands as a prophetic witness to an entire generation, crying God is still *"Emanuel"* - He's God With Us! He is with us in the here and now, and the weight of His presence and the fire that you carry demonstrates this kingdom reality.

Jesus said, *"The lamp of the body is the eye. Therefore, when your eye is good, your whole body also is full of light."* (Luke 11:34) The word *"good"* in the Greek is *"haplous"*, which literally means to be singular in one's focus. In other words, Jesus is saying, when your eye is singular in its pursuit of Him and void of all other distractions, you are going to steward a burning heart, and in turn your whole body will be full of light!

It's no secret that we live in the midst of a culture that is drowning in distractions. Marketing agents are fighting for our eyes, and they understand that if they can capture and sustain our attention they can fuel and provoke our passions. Sadly, so many are consumed in the cyber and pseudo worlds of social media and pop culture. I'm not condemning them, but I want my passion and attention to be consumed by God alone. I don't want anything to steal or hinder my desire for His word and His glory! I want the eyes of my heart to have unbroken focus. I want my eyes fixed on the place of *gazing upon the beauty of the Lord!* (Psalm 27:4)

We must focus our lives. That to which we consistently surrender our eyes, reveals what our heart truly burns for. We need to ask God for the abundance of grace, that we might live with a consecrated and singular eye, so that we might in turn steward a burning heart. You can zealously burn with the Spirit! Remember, what we behold we will surely become.

I believe that you are called to be a burning lamp, as witness to this generation. I believe that you desire to live a consecrated life fully pleasing unto The Lord. I pray that God will give you covenant friends who will burn with you and run passionately with you to ignite our world with His Presence and Love! The gifts and blessings that we pray for in life come in the packages of other people. Our job is to recognize and discern when those gifts are presented, so that we can be the recipients of God's grace and goodness, in and through them. May you identify your band of brothers or *family of fire*! To those that believe they just need God alone, they are terribly mistaken. You need God, and you need His people in your life! May you find a company of burning hearts just like yours! I dare you to be consumed with God and see how He will move to transform your life into the realm of the miraculous, the amazing and the extraordinary. May your burning heart become a catalyst for cities and nations to be set ablaze by the fire of The Lord!

CHAPTER THREE

SET YOUR WORLD ON FIRE

"I came to bring fire on the earth, and how I wish it were already set ablaze!" - Jesus
Luke 12:49 | NIV

A few years ago, I was ministering in a dynamic downtown Church in Stockholm, for a dear friend of ours. After finishing up our morning leadership session, a young Swedish man came up to me trembling - his eyes filled with tears, he shared that while I was imparting, he had felt the same fire that had fallen on him many years before, when God called him into the ministry. He had only been to America one time with his parents, many years ago, for a revival in Pensacola, Florida – a place called Brownsville. I smiled and told him that my wife and I had been there many years ago as well. He asked me for prayer. His request was focused – *"more fire"*! This young man was what my friend Tommy Tenney calls a *"God Chaser"*. *A God Chaser is one whose passion for God's presence presses him to chase the impossible, in hopes that the uncatchable might catch him.* His hunger was beautiful and pure. It moved me! When I laid my hands upon him, God powerfully and dramatically touched him in what

I often refer to as *"power encounters"*. He was vibrating under the Presence of God so strongly that it appeared as though he was being electrocuted. The unseen hand of God was dribbling him like a basketball against the floor. These kind of encounters are holy, and I have seen them all over the planet, as The Unstoppable and Unquenchable One comes to fill and ignite the human heart with love and power!

Notice the young man's words. He said he felt the *same* fire that he encountered many years ago! In the Greek, this word for *same fire* is "homothumadon". The word is a compound from *homos* meaning "same or together," and *thumos* meaning "passion, fierceness, heat, or glow." Joining these concepts together, the word can be understood as the same burning of heart, or same heart passion. The holy fire that he encountered did not originate in a revival in Florida. Though it's the *same fire,* its' roots can be traced all the way back to an upper room in Jerusalem on the day of Pentecost.

Bearing Witness of Jesus

In Acts 2, The Holy Spirit invaded Jerusalem and baptized these believers with fire to set the earth ablaze!

"When the Day of Pentecost had fully come, they were all with one accord in one place. And suddenly there came a sound from heaven, as of a rushing mighty wind, and it filled the whole house where they were sitting. Then there appeared to them divided tongues, as of fire, and one sat upon each of them. And they were all filled with the Holy Spirit and began to speak with other tongues, as the Spirit gave them utterance."
Acts 2:1-4 | NKJV

God longs for every human heart to be set on fire with His love and power! To be filled with the Spirit of God and baptized of His holy fire is a glorious wonder. It is truly incomprehensible that The God of all the universe, known and unknown, chose to make His abiding place within the human heart. The abiding presence of the Holy Spirit is one of the most crucial and distinguishing characteristics of a Christian. The prophet Joel declared, *"And afterward, I will pour out my Spirit on all people. Your sons and daughters will prophesy, your old men will dream dreams, your young men will see visions. Even on my servants, both men and women, I will pour out my Spirit in those days. I will show wonders in the heavens..."* (Joel 2:28-23 NKJV) To be filled with the Spirit of God is to be filled with dreams and visions that are far too compelling to ignore!

After Jesus had risen from the dead and was upon the earth 40 days, giving witness of His resurrection, the last thing He commanded His disciples, before ascending into heaven, was that they were: *"... not to depart from Jerusalem, but to wait for the Promise of the Father, "which," He said, "you have heard from Me; for John truly baptized with water, but you shall be baptized with the Holy Spirit not many days from now."* (Acts 1:4 NKJV)

Acts 1:8 | NKJV

"But you shall receive power when the Holy Spirit has come upon you; and you shall be witnesses to Me in Jerusalem, and in all Judea and Samaria, and to the end of the earth."

Jesus' command contained two absolute essentials, "you shall receive power" and "you shall be witnesses unto Me". It is essential for a witness or ambassador of Jesus to carry spiritual power, because without it, we can accomplish nothing. Furthermore, spiritual power that does not give witness to Jesus has no purpose. Every spiritual gift endowed by The Holy Spirit, including speaking in tongues, is given for the believer to bear witness of the saving work of Jesus through His cross and resurrection. Whenever the church begins to emphasize spiritual gifts apart from Jesus as the centerpiece, we are in trouble. But equally important, I have seen a notable extreme in the Body of Christ (especially in our generation) in which Christians have the tendency to place far too little emphasis on the Holy Spirit and spiritual gifts, which robs the church of its' inheritance of power. There is nothing more miserable than a Christian trying to live the Christian life without really knowing the joy and power of the Holy Spirit.

Jesus' commission to us is the same commission he gave to his disciples before His resurrection: *"And He said to them, "Go into all the world and preach the gospel to every creature. He who believes and is baptized will be saved; but he who does not believe will be condemned.*

And these signs will follow those who believe: In My name they will cast out demons; they will speak with new tongues; they will take up serpents; and if they drink anything deadly, it will by no means hurt them; they will lay hands on the sick, and they will recover." (Mark 16:15-18 | NKJV)

In this commission we see again the essentials that bear witness unto Jesus – His presence and power – with signs following those who believe. Our commission as believers is to preach to all nations the gospel of the kingdom, with presence and demonstrations of power. The preaching of *"repentance and remission of sins"* prepares the way for *"the promise of The Father"*, which is the Holy Spirit. On the day of Pentecost, they were *"endued with power from on high"*! Acts 2:4 brings clarity that the initial evidence of the presence of the Holy Spirit in power was that the believers" began to *"speak with other tongues, as the Spirit gave them utterance"*. This was the catalyst for preaching the gospel to thousands gathered in Jerusalem for the festival. This spiritual power and baptism was given for bearing witness to Jesus!

After Jesus' ascension from the Mount of Olives in Jerusalem, 10 days later, Acts chapter 2 gives us this supernatural and marvelous account...

*"When the Day of Pentecost had fully come, they were all with one accord in one place. And suddenly there came **a sound from heaven, as of a rushing mighty wind, and it filled the whole house where they were sitting**. Then **there appeared to them divided tongues, as of fire, and one sat upon each of them**. And **they were all filled with the Holy Spirit and began to speak with other tongues**, as the Spirit gave them utterance.*

*And there were dwelling in Jerusalem Jews, devout men, from every nation under heaven. And when **this sound occurred, the multitude came together, and were confused, because everyone heard them speak in his own language**. Then **they were all amazed and marveled**, saying to one another, "Look, are not all these who speak Galileans? And how is it that we hear, each in our own language in which we were born? Parthians and Medes and Elamites, those dwelling in Mesopotamia, Judea and Cappadocia, Pontus and Asia, Phrygia and Pamphylia, Egypt and the parts of Libya adjoining Cyrene, visitors* *from Rome, both Jews and proselytes, Cretans and Arabs – we hear them speaking in our own tongues the wonderful works of God." So they were* **all amazed and perplexed**, *saying to one another,* **"Whatever could this mean?"** *Others mocking said,* **"They are full of new wine."**

But Peter, standing up with the eleven, raised his voice and said to them, "Men of Judea and all who dwell in Jerusalem, let this be known to you, and heed my words. **For these are not drunk, as you suppose***, since it is only the third hour of the day.* **But this is what was spoken by the prophet Joel:** *'And it shall come to* **pass in the last days, says God, That I will pour out of My Spirit on all flesh; Your sons and your daughters shall prophesy, Your young men shall see visions, Your old men shall dream dreams. And on My menservants and on My maidservants I will pour out My Spirit in those days; And they shall prophesy.**
Acts 2:2-13 | NKJV

Perhaps more than ever before in our generation, we must encounter the outpouring of the Holy Spirit! The world needs more than inspirational sermons. I believe it is longing for the authentic power of God to be put on display. There must be power that transforms lives! As long as we depend on human wisdom, we will always fall short – victims of the forms and formulas of godliness without power. We live within an epic confrontation of the powers of darkness and the powers of light. The Church cannot rely on human wisdom, ingenuity and natural understanding to persuade the masses. What we need is real spiritual power – the power of The Holy Spirit! Jesus said, "…and you shall receive "power" when the Holy Spirit comes upon you!" His power is the true source of healing - miracles and wonders! I can fully expect a life of miracles and the supernatural because the Holy Spirit has come and filled my inner man!

The Apostle Paul understood the source of the true power and authority in The Spirit of God – The revelation of Christ and Him crucified:

"For the message of the cross is foolishness to those who are perishing, but to us who are being saved it is the power of God…

For Jews request a sign, and Greeks seek after wisdom; but we preach Christ crucified, to the Jews a stumbling block and to the Greeks[b] foolishness, 24 but to those who are called, both Jews and Greeks, Christ the power of God and the wisdom of God."
1 Corinthians 1:18, 22-24 | NIV

"And I, brethren, when I came to you, did not come with excellence of speech or of wisdom declaring to you the testimony of God. For I determined not to know anything among you except Jesus Christ and Him crucified. I was with you in weakness, in fear, and in much trembling. 4 And my speech and my preaching were not with persuasive words of human wisdom, but in demonstration of the Spirit and of power, that your faith should not be in the wisdom of men but in the power of God."
1 Corinthians 2:1-5 | NKJV

Paul specifically pointed to the unveiling of spiritual power as testimony that bore witness to Jesus: *" For I will not dare to speak of any of those things which Christ has not accomplished through me, in word and deed, to make the Gentiles obedient— in mighty signs and wonders, by the power of the Spirit of God, so that from Jerusalem and round about to Illyricum I have fully preached the gospel of Christ."* Romans 15:18&19 | NKJV

Paul was one of the most profound and brilliant intellectuals of his day, yet his secret was the *"demonstration of the Spirit and of power"*. He realized that human wisdom by itself would never lead to spiritual wisdom or knowledge of the deeper things of God. Only the Holy Spirit can impart that wisdom. Like Paul, let it be said of you, that your witness and *testimony provokes obedience* to others and that you *fully preach the gospel in mighty signs and wonders, by the power of the Spirit of God!* Power points to something greater – its' Source!

When this *sound* on the day of Pentecost occurred, look how the multitude in Jerusalem responded. They were amazed (to affect with great wonder), they marveled (surprise, astonished, awe) and were perplexed – (uncertain, puzzled, troubled)! Wow! If you haven't noticed, you don't hear people describing Church with language of being awed and puzzled by The Presence of God! Where is the wonder? Where is the glory?

Today we hear words like: boring, soporific, dull, pointless and uninteresting. We've been taken prisoner with our hour-long services for the masses – all nice and neatly packaged, over-structured and designed for the mechanical forms of religion. Sadly, most of what is done in our churches doesn't even seem to need explanation. It can be simply obtained with human ability and with very little, if any, anointing whatsoever.

We need tangible signs that point to the Source in our midst! Isn't it a pity that we have been satisfied to celebrate what natural abilities can accomplish? Weak leaders avoid the supernatural at all cost. The gravest cost is wasting their lives and their high calling at the altar of being a *respectable minister*. God is going to show up in America again! He wants His Church back, and He's going to get what He wants! He's tired of the games and the cotton candy we are feeding the masses! He's coming to torch all the silly religious systems and fill His people with Holy Fire!

Ten days in obedience to the words of Jesus to go and pray – "… *watch and wait for Holy Spirit until you are endued with power from on high*" – and look what happened! This is God's idea of a great day at church – filling His disciples with His heart to overflowing, so that the entire City thought that they were drunk and beside themselves. Is it any wonder why men have fought so hard for control? Is it any wonder why leaders have feared yielding control to the Holy Spirit? It might get messy. It might get controversial. I have found far too many leaders that do not value wonder and mystery. They've chosen to play it "safe". Man values mechanics and structure, but God values full possession!

On the Day of Pentecost, the Church was born of His Spirit and became a *sign and a wonder!* Obviously, we understand that the Church is not a building or denomination. It wasn't the upper room of Jerusalem that was holy, but rather the invasion of people being enveloped and filled with the awe and wonder of His manifest presence! A sign is that which points you to greater reality. When you go to Chick-fil-A, you don't park your car and sit under the sign out by the road. The sign points you inside for the substance. A wonder is that which cannot be explained. It takes spiritual understanding to comprehend spiritual things. In Romans 8:5-8, the Apostle Paul speaks of this, *"For those who live according to the flesh set their minds on the things of the flesh, but those who live according to the Spirit, the things of the Spirit. For to be carnally minded is death, but to be spiritually minded is life and peace. Because the carnal mind is enmity against God; for it is not subject to the law of God, nor indeed can be. So then, those who are in the flesh cannot please God."*

1 Corinthians 2:14 | HNV
"But the natural man does not receive the things of the Spirit of God, for they are foolishness to him; nor can he know them, because they are spiritually discerned."

People frequently criticize what they can't understand. In case you didn't notice, the Scriptures make it clear that others were *mocking* what they were seeing. Peter had to explain the phenomena of the Spirit. And notice that he had to explain that the people were not drunk as the multitude supposed. Why did they think they were drunk or intoxicated? Because they were inebriated in The Spirit! The Holy Spirit came and took over! He didn't come and just bless their prayer meeting. He took over!

We may not like to admit it, but I believe that our perspective and that of God, as to how we function as a Church, are worlds apart. Our gatherings together should be the most exhilarating gatherings on the face of the earth! The Church is God's chosen anomaly. An anomaly is a *departure from the normal or common order, common form and rule. One that is peculiar, irregular, abnormal, or difficult to classify.* I'm hungry for the Church to become rallying points of supernatural encounter! Rallying points of radical unbridled worship and dispensers of hope and power! I long to see our generation, by the millions, baptized with The Spirit and fire! It is no secret that there is an anti-Christ spirit that is working diligently to seduce the people of God. Leaders are especially under attack, deceived into thinking that they must keep the church tame, respectable, and manageable. It's a controlling spirit masquerading as *order* in the church. Unfortunately, it's rooted in the fear of man. Before we moved to Florida, to pioneer a Church, I was posed this question by one of my mentors: *"Brian, do you know who controls the Church? Whoever the Pastor is afraid of is who controls the church. You just continue to fear The Holy Spirit and you'll be just fine."* He was right!

Pastors all too often vacillate between attempting to please the people - maintaining respect in the community – and truly serving God. Now don't misunderstand what I'm saying. God gives a platform to righteous men and women to serve and love their cities. But if we're not watchful and vigilant, it is possible to fall into the trap of making our churches nothing more than community centers - tame and palatable for the masses. I want to remind us of what Paul wrote in 1 Thessalonians 5:19, **"Do not quench the Spirit"**. To "quench" means: to put the fire out, to suppress, squelch, dissolve, to put an end to, or destroy. Do not grieve and quench God, The Holy Spirit! The Holy Spirit is every bit as much a part of God as the Father and Son. Paul goes on in v. 20…*"do not despise prophecies!"* I hear the Lord saying – Keep the fire burning!

Holy Spirit + U = Winning Combo!

Amos 3:7 | NKJV (Parenthesis mine)
"Surely the Lord God does nothing, unless He reveals His secret counsel to His servants (friends) the prophets."

When I was a teenager, this scripture from Amos intrigued me. I've always thought it was notable that Jesus called His prophets His friends. From a very tender age, and throughout my life, I have committed myself to this divine pursuit, to be a *friend* of God and to make my heart available, that He might share His secrets with. I'm not a prophet, but I can tell you that God really enjoys talking with me and sharing His special desires with me. He does with you too!

Years ago, Gary Chapman wrote the book, "The Five Love Languages". It's a great book. Gary shares that one of the love languages is *quality time or time well spent*. This love language is all about giving the other person your undivided attention. I have come to learn that God is the Person who treasures us most and He loves time well spent with you and me. Isn't that amazing? What is profound is that the more time we spend with Him, the more we are transformed into His very likeness. In fact, that is our destiny, to be conformed into the image of His Son. It has been said, *"that which we behold we will become"*. Remarkably, God desires to share His intimate emotions and feelings with His friends. It's mindboggling to consider that He desires to share His will, intentions and dreams with us. Yes, God has emotions and feelings. Have you thought about that lately? The God of the Universe desires friendship with each and every one of us and He desires to spend quality time in sharing His very essence.

Jesus told us: *"No longer do I call you servants, for a servant does not know what his master is doing; but I have called you friends, for all things that I heard from My Father I have made known to you. You did not choose Me, but I chose you and appointed you that you should go and bear fruit, and that your fruit should remain, that whatever you ask the Father in My name He may give you."* (John 15:15&16 ESV)

The more that we spend quality time with The Lord, the more He discloses His ways and his plans to heal, restore and rescue broken lives. God has life transforming things to say to people, and His words are full of spirit and life. You're called to be His messenger. You're His partner and conduit of transformation. Flowing with the Holy Spirit is the greatest adventure, and the more we obey His voice, the more we will see tangible results of God's power.

Gods' friends change the present world! The new breed pioneers and revivalists, whom God is raising up even now, are those who treasure friendship and time well spent with God. They are not transient wandering souls, for His Presence has become their permanent residence as they release the power of Jesus throughout the earth. Their delight is found is filling the earth with His power and testimony. For the past twenty years of my life I have burned with this conviction - to be a man that hosts and releases the presence of

God everywhere I go. Everyday has become an experiment of partnering with The Holy Spirit, to impart His life in word and action. I want to be a man who apprehends *greater works*! How about you?

Bill Johnson, a friend and awesome pioneer in this present move of God, often says, *"We owe people an encounter with God."* I couldn't agree more!

Greater Works!

*"...He who believes in Me, **the works that I do he will do also**; and **greater works** than these he will do, because I go to My Father." – Jesus*
John 14:12 | NKJV

I wonder, *do we really believe this*? I mean: really? Let your anointed imagination take flight. What could the Lord do through, you if you would only believe? Open your heart and mind to His ideas and plans to unveil His glory through you. This is a prophecy and a promise from Jesus. I would encourage you to let it envelop your expectations for the rest of your life! Prophecy and promises are apprehended by those who believe and contend for *greater works*. Signs and wonders follow those who believe. If you want a boring Christian life, choose the method of doubt and unbelief. If you want the abundant experiential life of miracles, I encourage you to let your faith rise, and partner with the Holy Spirit for the seemingly impossible. Jesus never would have given this promise of *greater works* if it were not possible.

What "impossibilities" will God direct you to transform, in bringing heaven to earth? Will you heal the sick? There's no sickness in heaven. Will you believe for God to use you to crush and destroy disease? There's no disease in heaven. Will you raise the dead? I mean, really? Will you disciple Nations? Will you restore marriages from the brink of despair? Will you give hope and dreams to those who have been afraid to believe again? Will you reveal forgiveness and healing to the woman that has hated herself all her life for the baby she aborted? Will you expel demons from the tormented teenager who cuts her wrist each night to drink her own blood? Will you bring economic and financial freedom to those bound in a spirit of poverty? Will you bring deliverance and freedom to the homosexual who is bound by unclean and perverted spirits? Will you rescue the rich from their false loves and idols? What will these *greater works* look like when you believe? God has chosen you to bring His victory to this world. He has commissioned every believer to do what is seemingly impossible. Jesus is still saying, "Follow Me". You won't be sorry when you do!

The Kingdom

Jesus taught us to pray in this manner, *"Father, Your kingdom come. Your will be done on earth as it is in heaven."* (Matthew 6:10) Jesus would have never told us to pray such an unprecedented prayer if it were not possible. Remember, Jesus only said what the Father said. (John 5:19&20) This tells us that this desire was emanating from the Father's heart. He longs for His children to ask in this way, because this is the prayer he desires to answer! God's desire is that we release heaven here in the earth. It is possible and readily available for us to access. Again, Jesus would have never told us to pray in this way, if it were not possible. Those who tasted and know the goodness of the Father's heart can become a catalyst to release heaven!

When we pray for His kingdom to come, we are asking for His divine order, His unending supply, and the all-surpassing power of His world to invade ours. As His ambassadors, we carry our King's commands, and we have the privilege of representing His world and releasing heaven's resources into this present age.

Jesus said that *this gospel of the kingdom will be preached in all the world, and then the end will come.* The gospel of the kingdom, according to Jesus, was revealed by proclaiming *the kingdom is at hand* and then demonstrating its dominion through the miraculous. *"For the kingdom of God is not just a lot of talk, but it's living in God's power."* (1 Corinthians 4:20) The message of the *kingdom* – literally meaning, *the King's domain* – heralds that His lordship and authority is over all things, and through the demonstration of signs and wonders, God releases heaven to earth. Can you image when a generation fully believes this and demonstrates the gospel of the kingdom as Jesus did? It's going to happen! When believers awaken to what is available to them, they will leave powerless Christianity behind! The *kingdom is at hand* – within reach and available now - to those who believe!

If this beautiful kingdom is available in the here and now for *greater works*, how is it that most of the church world is so comfortably content and satisfied with so little of God in their midst? God's desire is that every believer and church should be bursting with supernatural power and exploits! His power is what revolutionizes the world around us. Miracles and wonders will become normal, where courageous faith lays hold of them. Faith draws from the unseen realm accessing answers and solutions into this realm. Faith is the conduit that releases heavenly transactions. The kingdom of God is always within reach by those who believe it, seek it, expect it and receive it for our present world. Go set your world on fire!

Compassion Releases Miracles

Jesus said, "Come, follow me and I will teach you how to fish for people."
(Mark 1:7 | NLT)

I was sick for weeks from a cold that grew worse. We were newly married, and Bren had told me time and again, *maybe you should just go to the doctor's office.* After three grueling weeks, I finally decided to heed the voice of wisdom – Bren's.

After filling out the paperwork at the walk-in clinic, I waited patiently...and waited some more...and then some more. After an hour and a half had passed, I was so frustrated that I was about to leave. That's when the nurse came out and pleasantly welcomed me back to my room. It was there that I would wait for nearly another hour for the Doctor's arrival. Finally, the Doctor arrived and began to ask me about the symptoms I had been experiencing. After a few minutes into the conversation, he asked me what I did for a living. I told him that I was a Pastor. Suddenly, there was a shift in the atmosphere and I could feel his animosity immediately.

As he continued to examine me with breathing tests and a throat culture for strep, He began to tell me what he thought of preachers. He was brazen and quite condescending, as he took time to share what he thought of the organized Church - Christians and ministers in general. It was very awkward and uncomfortable. I could tell he was speaking out of a place of deep offense and hurt. As I listened to him, I was honestly so frustrated that I started complaining to the Lord. Why should I have to sit and listen to his berating of Christians? I was so taken back by his boldness and animosity. I thought to myself, *Jesus, I'm your friend...this is your buddy, Brian, remember me? I'm your servant needing healing...why do I need to sit here and tolerate this moron?* Furthermore, I really didn't like this guy touching me.

After his examination, the Doctor instructed me to wait patiently and go ahead and put my shirt and coat back on. I waited...and I waited some more. I went out into the hallway to stretch my legs and walk the hall, because I couldn't sit anymore in the room. When I walked down the hallway I happened to look into the room that was next to mine. There was an older couple sharing an intimate conversation. She was lying in the bed and he was standing near her, bent down - his forehead touching hers. Their faces were close together and they were crying. He was whispering his affections for her. As I passed their room I felt the Holy Spirit pull the plug on my tub of frustrations and felt a sudden deluge of His compassions towards this couple. As I quietly began to pray I felt deep waves of compassion begin to well up within me. I passed the room slowly again and watched them. I watched the man lovingly caressing her face and rubbing her hair. It was then I saw the large tumor on the side her neck. The growth was large – impossible to miss. I passed another time and began to pray for this woman, releasing heaven's atmosphere, summoning Holy Spirit and the ministering angels to touch this couple. I went back into my room and began to pray fervently. I was feeling the Lord's deep waves of compassion and love for them. I prayed earnestly with faith for her healing and deliverance. Within about 40 minutes the nurse and Doctor came back into the room to let me know what I had and what my prescription was. The three of us exited the room together. The doctor walked to a medical widow in the hall to fill out some papers, while the nurse went into the office. As I began to walk down the hall, the elderly couple exited their room as well. The gentleman was escorting his wife slowly to the drinking fountain. She had a small cup in her hand and was holding her neck where the growth was with her other hand. Her husband was gently assisting her across the hallway. I felt waves of compassion hit me again, and I began to pray, as I went to pass them. Deliberately looking for a place of contact, I gently touched her elbow and prayed silently. I walked onward to the main foyer to pay for my visit. As I was writing the check, I heard the woman cry out from the hallway - IT'S GONE, IT'S GONE! I heard a bit of commotion, so I walked over to take a look. The doctor and nurse were standing with the elderly couple. Perplexed! The growth on her neck had completely disappeared and the woman and her husband were crying, saying to each other, "It's gone!" It was completely gone! I was shocked! I stepped back in the doorway, so the Doctor wouldn't see me. Well, he did.

He ran down the hallway to where I was standing and just stared at me with this perplexed look on his face. I didn't say a word. I just turned and walked out of the clinic. At that moment, I too was healed. I didn't go get a prescription that day. I sat in the car overwhelmed by God's loving kindness! I cried. I laughed. I thought, "Lord you are so good! You brought me here at this time just for them." That afternoon He spoke so clearly to me that when I am moved with His compassions, miracles can be released. I went home to share this with Bren. What a day of celebration it was! This was the day that raised the bar in my expectations for the supernatural! Impossibilities will bow to the name of Jesus, when we simply learn to yield to His compassions and release faith.

In His Presence

It was a beautiful day on the Adriatic Sea in Pescara, Italy. Bren and I were ministering during a weeklong conference along with a friend of ours - who is a notable prophet. Pastors and ministers from all over Italy, Southern and Western Europe had come hungry to encounter the Lord. One morning, in a Q&A session, an Italian

Pastor asked Don a sensitive question that moved me deeply. He explained his grief about how many of the American ministries that had come throughout the years to Italy had made them feel inferior - as if they needed the American's anointing. Don's response was humble and insightful. He first repented for the arrogance of ministries of days gone by – embarrassed that that had fostered and broadcasted such narcissism. He then explained that we were there not to give them "our anointing", but we were there on assignment to help uncap and activate the pulsating and living river of God within them!

That afternoon, Bren and I went up to our hotel room, and I began to pray for wisdom for the night session. The Lord was letting me feel His heart and his grief over the performance of man, often short circuiting and hindering the life-giving Spirit of God. Bren and I talked about the mentality of ministries that have brought hurt and detriment to the Body of Christ. As we were praying for the night rally and I was preparing my message, I asked the Lord to do something significant. I prayed that He would take all the attention and emphasis off of me as the speaker and pour out His Spirit upon us! God answered my humble prayer!

That night, the Presence of The Lord filled that auditorium in a remarkable way and it kept getting thicker and richer. Worship was intoxicating. I could smell the fragrance of His Presence while I was speaking. I was watching a little boy in the crowd who was with his parents, also Pastors. The Presence of The Lord was on him strong, and he was trembling and weeping quietly in his chair. Each time I got near him I kept experiencing a greater intensity of the heart of God. After about 30 minutes into the message, I asked the mother to bring her son forward. The mother took hold of him and brought him into the altar area. She introduced him as, "Hons" and said he was 8 years of age. Through my interpreter, I asked if the man sitting next to her was her husband? He was sitting with his arms across his chest looking angry and uncomfortable. She said, "Yes, he is. He's a Pastor and he does not believe in all of these manifestations - people falling down, the shaking and laughter." I asked her if I could pray for Hons and she agreed. I simply began to bless what Holy Spirit had initiated and asked for increase - more love, more fire, more power. The glory of God was tangible and intensifying upon this precious boy. I began to lead him through the auditorium to impart to these ministers, but they could barely get near Hons as the glory swept them down into power encounters! Within about 30 minutes, hundreds of ministers were laying in piles on the floor, being filled with The Spirit! They were weeping, laughing and caught up with The Lord!

My attention was drawn to the back of the auditorium as groups of people from off the streets were *randomly* finding their way into the meeting. In particular, I noticed that 3 transvestites had made their way in and were sitting on the edge of their seats, watching what was taking place. As I led Hons up one of the aisles to pray for others, we got caught in a "hot spot" or a "hot pocket" of the presence of God. The joy of the Lord was being poured out. It was outrageous and ecstatic joy! There was a notable increase of the Presence that came in like a wave. We must have remained in the aisle for about 20 minutes.

As I guided Hons to the front near the stage, I noticed two significant things. His father had made his way up into the altar area and was weeping. The three transvestites had come forward and were bowing at the altar, sobbing. I directed Hons to his father where he humbly opened his arms and bowed down for his son to pray for him. Both he and his father were swept to the floor under the weightiness of The Presence. It was absolutely beautiful.

At the same time, the glory of God washed these three men clean. I beheld a miracle transformation right before my eyes. They were delivered from all demonic bondage and torment. I don't feel it would be appropriate in this book to share everything I witnessed, but God washed these men from darkness, and it was profound and majestic...it was beautiful and fearful. Friends, in His presence, nothing, absolutely nothing is impossible!

Hons ~ One more time!

A few weeks after we returned from Italy, Bren and I were ministering back in Springfield, Illinois. The altars were packed with several hundred people, seeking prayer. I was watching the ministry team from the stage. There was a young mother standing against the steps who motioned for me to come over to pray for her and her son. She introduced herself and her eight-year old. His name was HONS! Wow! She told me that he was born deaf in his left ear and asked if I would pray for him. When she said "Hons", the compassion of Jesus welled up in my spirit. I laid my hand on the boy's ear, and it was completely opened and healed! The two of them fell into each other's arms weeping and celebrating! Hon's face was aglow with tears of joy! I love seeing Jesus show up! He is the same yesterday, today and forever!

When Revival Crashes Into You

It was a beautiful afternoon. Bren and I had enjoyed a day together at the beach to rest, get refreshed, and soak in some premium Florida sunshine. We were on our way home from Lido Key and were sitting at a red light. As we were sitting there talking, I happened to glance into the rearview mirror only to find a woman coming up right behind us, and it was clear, that she was not stopping! I only had time to stretch out my arm over my wife and shout "hold on". The woman plowed right into the back of our car. I asked Bren if she was ok, and she said she was. I was fine too. I turned off the car and got out to assess the damage and check on the lady. The woman's car was totaled. I was so frustrated. Bren walked over to the side of the road to call the police. I went to the woman's car, opened her door and shut off the vehicle. She was crying and in a lot of pain as her left arm was clearly broken. I helped her out of the car and made sure that everyone was ok. I was so aggravated with the woman and the situation.

As I walked her over to Bren and waited for the police to arrive, I moved from being completely aggravated to feeling compassion for this woman. I began to pray silently for her and for her arm. I also began to speak to her bone to be set and healed. The police arrived on the scene and the officer began to ask about the accident. I noticed his name badge – Officer, HEAVEN. I'm not kidding! Officer Heaven. I laughed, and asked him about his name, and he shared a few good laughs with Bren and me. I continued to pray for the woman silently, as she was still pretty shaken up by the whole event. To my utter surprise, I looked down at her arm, which I had been gently holding, and realized that the bone had moved back into place. It was set and healed! Oh my, oh my - JESUS! I wanted to shout and rejoice, but instead I said to her, well, look there...it looks like your arm is going to be just fine. She looked down at her arm, looked at me, looked back at her arm, look back up at me, looked down at her arm – at this point – that large mouth bass face took shape...haha! Large mouth bass? Come on now. Gaping mouth? There, you got it!

Her response startled me. She said, I know who you are! I know who you are! My wife and I looked at one another, thinking... hmmm, this is odd. She said, "You're Pastor Brian, I know who you are now"...She went on..."In 1999 I was going through the worst time of my life and walked through a brutal divorce. I was depressed, drinking heavily, on pills and at times suicidal. I lost it all. I came to a Church in Springfield, Illinois that was hosting a revival, and you were there preaching. That was the night you gave the altar call, and I gave my heart to the Lord. I gave my life to Jesus that night and was delivered from every affliction and substance abuse." Whoa! Bren and I were stunned! Officer Heaven was stunned! So many years later, and here was this woman, now sharing her testimony of salvation and the goodness of God. The beauty of the Lord turned a terrible situation into an encounter of praise and thanksgiving. We prayed with her and loved on her, as Officer Heaven stood silently observing. Always look for God to move into any situation. Be sensitive and compassionate and remember - compassion is the key that gives us access to miracles!

The Rubik's Cube & The Potter's Hands

We were ministering in Columbus, Ohio for a week of meetings. I asked a gentleman to step into the aisle for prayer, and as he did, the Holy Spirit showed me a unique prophetic picture. I saw the Potter's wheel spinning and a Rubik's Cube coming down over the wheel. Then I saw The Potter's hands descending upon the cube aligning all the colors that were disarrayed and placing them in correct position and order.

101

For those that may not be familiar with a Rubik's Cube, it's a game that hit mainstream popularity in the 1980's. The cube is a small 3-D multicolored combination puzzle. Frankly, it drove me crazy trying to perfect that game as a teenager!

I began to prophecy over this man, that The Lord was placing his life into His hands. He would shape him upon the Potter's wheel, just as in *Jeremiah 18*. God was going to reshape, reform and align all that had tragically been out of place in his life. He would be brought to a place of perfection and wholeness and that the Lord would restore and heal his body.

Later that afternoon over lunch, the Pastor told us how Jay had been in a horrific accident on a construction site years ago, which nearly took his life. He was married and had a family, but the accident robbed him of being able to function normally. His disabilities were vast and kept him from so many things, which we take for granted. He was unable to enjoy his wife intimately, drive a car, read properly and on and on.

That week, Bren and I saturated Jay and his family in prayer over and over again. I was so moved by his story, his spiritual hunger and his golden heart for God. Over the next five years, any time that Bren and I were ministering in the State of Ohio, I would look over the crowds. Time and time again, I would see Jay and his wife attending the meetings. Little by little he was getting restored in his mind and in his body. His wife faithfully drove him to the meetings and would find us even in obscure cities. Time and again, they came for prayer and to testify how God was restoring him more and more. Now, I hope you caught this. It was over 5 years of progressive restoration.

One night, I was ministering in Eastern Ohio and to my surprise one of my interns pointed out that Jay was in the crowd that night, but not his wife. That got my attention. Later in the evening, healings were breaking out with knees, backs, jaws and teeth. It was marvelous. I called Jay to come to the front of the Church and asked him what was happening and to testify what the Lord had been doing in him. Jay shared his story from the very beginning, starting with the accident on the construction site over 20 years ago.

He shared the prophetic word I had given him five years before and of the progressive miracle-work in his mind and body. And then he told us the miracle was complete. He had driven himself to the meeting that night! All things had been restored to him. That which the Lord began, He was faithful to complete! There wasn't a dry eye in the building, as the goodness of God was melting us like wax. The more Jay shared, the more people got healed that night through just the power of the testimony. Jay fell out under the weightiness of the God's Presence at the altar, so I went to work on something special that night.

I wanted to break the spirit of poverty that was destroying that local Church. I told the people that if they wanted to sow into Jay's life to get up and bring an offering forward to bless this miracle! You've never seen so much money! The people buried him in cash. The Pastor sat on the stage and wept. He had never seen so much money released in their congregation. It was a remarkable demonstration of love, and their extravagant giving was delivering a crushing blow to the poverty mentality and spirit, which had gripped that region! It was a breakthrough moment.

The associate Pastor's wife approached me in the altar area and shared what she felt led to do. She, and many of the women in the church, had just returned from a Joyce Meyer conference. At the conference, a woman she had never met before approached her and said the Lord had told her to give her a ring. The ring was a stunning 2.5 carat diamond! She had it appraised, and it was very valuable. While Jay was sharing his testimony, the Holy Spirit told the Pastor's wife to give that ring to Jay for his wife!

When Jay finally began to get up from the floor, my intern and a few ushers helped him make his way over to me. I introduced Jay to the Pastor's wife, and she told him the story and presented the ring to him. I had never seen a grown man cry so intensely! It was embarrassing. I didn't know what to do. I wanted to settle Jay down, but he went on and on. Finally, he gained his composure and these were Jay's words: *"Tomorrow is our 25th year wedding anni-versary! Because of the accident and all the things that I suffered over the years, I have never been able to bless my wife and give any of the things she deserves in our marriage - especially a ring this beautiful! I have always dreamed of giving her a ring like this!"*

Now I was weeping…The Pastor and I presented the money to Jay, and we watched him drive out of the church parking lot until his taillights were no longer visible. He drove back to Columbus that night loaded down with blessings! The Rubik's Cube was finally restored because of the Potter's healing hands!

I stood under the stars that night, out in the Church parking lot with Jesus, overflowing with thanksgiving…It's a wonderful life!

Victory over….A Skunk?

It was a Sunday afternoon in Batesville, Indiana. The church alter was packed with worshippers and the atmosphere was rich with spiritual hunger. After bringing the message that morning, the altars were filled with people pressing in before the Lord and desiring prayer. Suddenly, it was a scene like something right out of the Gospels. You remember the 4 friends who tore the roof off the house just to get their friend before Jesus? The crowd started parting as three men drug her down the aisle like a wilted flower before me. The usher yelled at me, *she's been sprayed by a skunk!* The atmosphere was quickly overcome with the horrendous smell! The woman had been sprayed, head to toe – mouth included! Her skin had turned ashen grey and she appeared asphyxiated! It was a horrible sight. I couldn't believe that these men had rushed her into the Church for prayer. You know, there is no course in Bible College - how to minister to "skunk victims"! LOL! None of my mentors, or my spiritual Dad, had ever spoken about how to deal with this kind of situation!

Suddenly, without even thinking about it, I heard myself boldly saying, *"Woman, take three deep breaths of the presence of God!"* I know, I know, what in world was I saying? It was a burst of faith. Nonetheless, with difficulty, she took a deep breath and blew out. She was so close to me that I nearly vomited. She breathed in a second breath and blew out. And then I said, *"Women, take one more and breath on me!"* She did! And when she blew out her third breath the smell had instantaneously vanquished, not only from her body, but from the entire Sanctuary! The congregation broke out in ecstatic celebration and joy! It was heavenly pandemonium! Guess who was the most shocked person in the room? That's right, me!

How do you explain this stuff? It's radical and it's real. It's God on display to meet our present conditions. His kingdom is close, closer than we have ever dared believed. Yet, He's right here and ready, *when we believe!* Thankfully, three deep breaths of The Presence of God can go a long way! Why don't you go ahead and take three deep breaths in faith right now for your own cleansing?

Words That Release Destiny

"It is the Spirit that gives life…the words that I speak to you, they are spirit, and they are life." - Jesus
John 6:63 | NKJV

It had been a very long and challenging day. I was pastoring at the time, and thought it would be good to unwind and refresh, before heading home for the evening. I went down to Sarasota Bay Park to enjoy the ocean, some sunshine and some alone time with The Lord. As I was sitting in the grass, enjoying the breeze and a new book, a young couple got out of their car behind me and began to walk in my direction. As I looked up to see them passing by, acknowledging them, I noticed they were a very attractive couple, probably in their late 20's, walking hand in hand.

The Lord spoke to me so clearly, *"Go tell them that they are to get married. Tell them that for all the trouble and adversity that they have experienced in their young lives, that God was going to give them the ultimate comeback and raise them up victoriously, and that they would have a ministry to young couples and families."* I'm not a stranger to releasing prophetic words, but the whole *"marriage"* word shocked me! Its just prophecy 101. You don't tell people whom they're supposed to marry! As a Pastor, I would be quick to correct or redirect anyone who gave that kind of a word at our church to a couple. I said, *"Lord, for real? Do I have to tell them that?"* His answer, *"Yes, Son."* He was overriding my prophecy 101 principle.

I went over and approached them as they were snuggling on a park bench, enjoying the ocean view. Politely introducing myself as a Pastor in Sarasota, I told them that as I was reading my book and saw them walking into the park, God spoke to me a beautiful word about their lives and their future. The moment I told them that The Lord said that they were to be married, both of them began to tremble and burst into streaming tears. The young lady gasped. Their response was quite dramatic. I humbly gave the word and told them that the Lord loved them. The young man said, "Pastor, we are Christians and this is a true miracle for us. We attend a Slavic/Russian church here in Sarasota, and we have been on a fast for the last three days, praying for clarity, if indeed it was the Lord's will for us to get married". They thanked me and said they would remember and treasure this day the rest of their lives. As I walked away and made my way back to my car, I sat watching this couple crying and holding one another. It was precious to behold. I sat and wept thanking the Holy Spirit for releasing such a special gift for them in this season of their journey. There is nothing like partnering with The Lord to release His heart for others.

Captives Set Free

"Heal the sick, cleanse the lepers, raise the dead, cast out demons. Freely you have received, freely give."
Matthew 10:8 | NKJV

The church was packed to almost beyond capacity. The overflow in the gymnasium was filled and God was on the move! There was a special rich Presence among us. This particular morning was a time we were setting apart to receive testimonies of healing and miracles.

We had a line of about 20 people in front of the Church giving witness of supernatural turnarounds and ultimate comebacks. They came with medical reports to confirm the goodness of God. Celebration was in the air!

I noticed that two young ladies, whom we did not recognize, had randomly come up and joined the end of the line, in hopes to making it to the microphone. I wasn't comfortable with what I was discerning, so I asked a few trusted ladies to go over and love on them. Within a few minutes I noticed somewhat of a stirring and a struggle starting to take place.

Suddenly, the ladies parted and I was eye to eye with a full-blown demon possessed girl. Her eyes had rolled back into her head and were protruding outward as she let out a roar. She shot up like a rocket off the stage and landed on her back. She then began to slither like a snake across the altar area. It was gross and angered me. I walked to stand over the top of this precious girl and commanded these demon spirits to come out of her in Jesus' name. What I saw and experienced next was extraordinary! Suddenly, I saw a terrifying fear in the eyes of this demon, as a mighty rushing wind came down over the top of me, hitting this girl and flushing her clean from every tormenting spirit. I asked my Dad and a few ladies to usher her and her friend into the prayer room, to love them and privately minister to them.

As I got back up on the stage, I could see the restlessness and the fear that this intense manifestation had created. The entire congregation was reeling. I was grieved that the enemy had humiliated that precious girl in such a way. I waited for a moment and then I simply asked those who were struggling with fear, because of what we had witnessed, to slip out of their seats and come down to the front so we might pray.

Without hesitation, people were getting up all over the auditorium and quickly making their way to the front. There may have been around forty who responded, and others made their way in from the gymnasium. As I came out from behind the pulpit to walk down the stairs to pray for them, suddenly and without warning the same mighty wind rushed from behind me. It was so strong, blowing my hair like in a windstorm. The wind hit these people and launched them into the air in every direction. Some were slammed to the ground. Others were blown backwards into the first and second rows. Some collapsed into each other. No one was left standing. The fear of The Lord gripped everyone and intercession and travail came gushing forth through the crowd. That morning we stayed for hours under a weighty blanketing of the glory of God. There was nothing more we could do but to lower and humble ourselves in the weight of His holiness.

What's especially beautiful, is that the two precious girls, one demon possessed, who had been hitch hiking across the country and turning tricks for truck drivers, were wonderfully saved and baptized in the Holy Spirit that day!

Freedom!

"For this purpose the Son of God was manifested, that He might destroy the works of the devil."
1 John 3:8 | NKJV

A few years ago, while still pastoring in Florida, we were hosting our annual fall conference, when one of the most notable deliverances I've ever seen occurred one afternoon. A mother approached Bren and me in the altar area. She shared that she and her daughter, with three close friends, had driven up from Ft. Lauderdale. Her daughter had fought her the entire trip, not wanting to come to the meetings, as she was backslidden and wanted nothing to do with the Church. Her daughter, then 21, had been running from the Lord, exposing herself to the occult and engaging in sexual sin.

During an afternoon session, I asked everyone to begin to pray for the person on the right and left – contending for healings and miracles. The daughter later shared, that she was so angry with her Mom that she didn't even want to sit next to her, so she put her Mom's three friends in between them. However, there was a man sitting to her right who turned to her during the prayer time and told her everything about her life! When the man finished, she heard and felt something burst and pop down in her belly and her mouth filled up with a strange wet jelly type substance. She took two fingers and reached inside her mouth to touch her tongue. When she pulled her hand back, she described a thick black ink-type substance running down her hand, startling her. Fear came over her. Suddenly, she felt an overwhelming peace, which steadied her. She reached back into her mouth again to touch her tongue once again with her other hand. This time, the black ink substance was gone! The girl had experienced a powerful deliverance from every demonic spirit, and her inner being was healed. She wept tears of thanksgiving as she held her Mother. I asked her who the man was who spoke to her. She said, "I don't know, he just disappeared. I don't see him anywhere".

Something happens to a person's spiritual DNA when they are exposed to the supernatural interventions of God! Miracles transform our thinking and expectations!

"But you shall receive power when the Holy Spirit has come upon you; and you shall be witnesses to Me in Jerusalem, and in all Judea and Samaria, and to the end of the earth." - JESUS

Go! Set your world on fire!

CHAPTER FOUR

GENERATIONS - FATHERING THE FIRE

Fathering is different than teaching. Teachers instruct you, but fathers love and build you. Authentic spiritual fathers and mothers go far beyond the ministry of the laying on of hands - they prefer the laying on of hearts!

When I was 25, Bren and I were running hard after God, lighting hearts and taking revival throughout America. One particular weekend, both of us were pretty excited to be "off" – so we could just be at home and relax. Jim Goll, a seasoned prophet that I have respected and admired for many years, was speaking that weekend at our home church. Jim ministered prophetically to me at the altar and told me that *God was going to make me into a father at a very young age. Not a natural father, but a spiritual father to many sons and daughters to come, and that I would begin to walk and function in the apostolic mantle at a young age…that I was marked for generations.* He was the first of three prophetic voices to give me the same word within six months. It was a remarkable and defining moment of awakening for me. In the years to follow, this prophetic word empowered and nourished my heart time and again, to stay the course through some of the most challenging and epic battles I would face in ministry. I began to discern early on that what was happening in my life was crucial, pivotal and prophetic - not only for my personal journey, but that my decisions and vows carried spiritual weight for those who were yet to come. I dared to pledge my life to hosting His Presence and bringing the Presence of God into the world, and God has unrelentingly dedicated Himself to bringing me into my prophetic destiny.

1 Timothy 1:18-19 | NLT

*"Timothy, my son, here are my instructions for you, **based on the prophetic words spoken about you earlier. May they help you fight well in the Lord's battles. Cling to your faith in Christ, and keep your conscience clean** (keep your integrity). **For some people have deliberately violated their consciences; as a result, their faith has been shipwrecked."***

Before I go any further, let me take some time to direct your attention to prophetic ministry. So far, in this book you have been seeing the unfolding and outworking of prophetic ministry helping to shape the course of my journey.

I absolutely believe in the power and significance of prophetic ministry, function, and specifically in this case, prophetic utterance. God reveals His mind specifically, within a particular context, as to what He wants to release and cause to unfold. Mindful of this, it is vital that we understand from the Scripture, that the utterance of a prophetic word is predicated on *"condition."* That is, all prophecy is *"conditional."* Failure to recognize that, real difficulty is sure to arise.

Think about Paul's words to his spiritual son Timothy. He was reminding him that these prophetic treasures were significant, and they would keep him on course and safe, as he navigated throughout the journey storms of life. Read it again.

"Timothy, my son, here are my instructions for you, based on the prophetic words spoken about you earlier. May they help you fight well in the Lord's battles. Cling to your faith in Christ, and keep your conscience clear (keep your integrity). For some people have deliberately violated their consciences; as a result, their faith has been shipwrecked."

112

Cling to your faith in Christ! In the King James Translation it says, in order to *"keep faith"* (which is a covenantal term and so often washed over and ignored in terms of its' significance) Timothy had to *"do"* something with the prophetic words spoken over him. Do not miss that! Many prophecies, because they are conditional, never come to pass for a number of reasons. It is extremely important, especially in this season, when people believe for words to come to pass, that they do not disqualify themselves because of an inaccurate understanding of how the prophetic function works from the standpoint of the Spirit. We must live responsibly.

For a moment, let's direct our attention to Paul's reference to Timothy as a "son" in the Gospel. To be a *son* or a *daughter* of Paul would be to follow Paul as Paul followed Christ. In essence, real disciples are sons and daughters. Please understand, it is only mature sons who are led by the Spirit; the rest live immature, need-driven lives. Paul makes that clear in Romans 8:14, that only the *"huios"* (Greek word for mature sons) are those who are led by the Spirit, all others are still enslaved to something else in their lives. It is what leads up to Romans 8:14 that enables us to understand the difference between being truly Spirit-led or being a slave of the law of sin and death.

In essence, if you lay claim, as a mature son or daughter of the Lord, to being the righteousness of God in Christ, your life has to be congruent with your confession. You have to live what you say, and walk what you talk. Your creeds and your deeds have to be in union, if not, you are what the Scripture calls carnal or "natural." In a day when much of what is being offered in commercialized Christianity is a grace without accountability, the fire of the Spirit is eventually going to consume whatever is not of Him, and those who do not bear fruit according to righteousness are, according to Jesus' own words, going to be thrown away as useless branches that do not abide in Him.

Grace is God's empowering Presence in your life, enabling you to live righteously and do those things that are in accordance with righteousness. You cannot separate righteousness from the glory of God. It is all about His reputation in the earth.

Son-ship is a major aspect of true discipleship, and a mature son or daughter is someone who, on a daily basis, as a follower of Jesus, is observing *all things* that He has *commanded*. True sons and daughters, real disciples, have no problem being "commanded" by Jesus. It is only natural and carnal Christians who buck at accountability and requirements, claiming "freedom in Jesus" as their excuse.

Paul says that where the Spirit of the Lord is there is liberty. However, taking that out of context, will lead to lawlessness, iniquity and idolatry. There is no liberty without His Lordship. There is no glory without His divine government in your life. A river has banks, and without those banks it would be a flood. Paul commands Timothy to fight the good faith, because *all prophecy is conditional*.

Our God is a consuming fire. Remember this, those who despise accountability and covenant faithfulness will reap the results of that in their lives. Those who love honor, loyalty and covenant faithfulness will be richly rewarded.

All prophecy is conditional. What should be very sobering is that every wonderful prophetic utterance we have heard will go unfulfilled without our active, intentional, deliberate pursuit as covenant sons and daughters; true disciples of Jesus. It is vital that you stay on course, and that we find Him worthy of any price that we must pay along the way.

There are many right now that are being groomed by The Spirit of the Lord to become *shepherds after God's own heart*, authentic spiritual fathers and mothers, who will guide and nourish with knowledge and understanding. (Jeremiah 3:15) The Apostle Paul wrote, *"For though you might have ten thousand instructors in Christ, yet **you do not have many fathers**; for in **Christ Jesus I have begotten you through the gospel**.* (1 Corinthians 4:15)

This is for sure a reality check! Teachers can produce classes for instruction, but they cannot produce a family. Many churches have become like schools, but they lack the warmth of the family room that fathers create. A true spiritual father will not seek his own gain in anything, but always the greater good of his spiritual children.

Paul says in 2 Corinthians 12:14 &15, *"I will not be a burden to you. I do not seek what is yours but you. Children are not responsible to save up for their parents, but parents for their children. I will most gladly spend and be expended for your souls"*. Those are the words of a true father. The truth is it cost Paul everything to be a father. He considered all that he had gained in life as rubbish compared to gaining Christ. He also considered it worth sacrificing everything in order to be a father to those whom he had brought to Christ.

There's no shortage of teachers everywhere. And praise God for them. But there must be those that will give themselves to the sculpting and shaping of The Potters hands to becoming fathers. Jesus came to reveal The Father. He came to give the world His Name – Abba – Papa, Daddy God. While the religious scribes were playing their church games, Jesus was true to His mission - revealing the Father's heart!

Shepherds After His Own Heart

Jeremiah 3:15 | NASB
*"And I will give you **shepherds according to My heart, who will feed you with knowledge and understanding."***

The Prophet, Jeremiah, was called to a backslidden Israel to return to the Father's heart and His marital covenant with Israel. God longed to be merciful to them and deliver them from their iniquity, transgressions and backslidings.

Jeremiah 3:12-15 | NKJV
'Return, backsliding Israel,' says the Lord; 'I will not cause My anger to fall on you. For I am merciful,' says the Lord; 'I will not remain angry forever.

Only acknowledge your iniquity, That you have transgressed against the Lord your God, And have scattered your charms To alien deities under every green tree, And you have not obeyed My voice,' says the Lord.

"Return, O backsliding children," says the Lord; "for I am married to you. I will take you, one from a city and two from a family, and

I will bring you to Zion. And I will give you shepherds according to My heart, who will feed you with knowledge and understanding."

In this word to Jeremiah, the language, *"according to my own heart"*, is lifted right out of God's declaration concerning David, 400 years prior. God had sought out His own king for Israel, as Saul's heart had become blackened and corrupted. God spoke concerning David in 1 Samuel 13:14, ...*"The Lord has sought for Himself a man after His own heart, and the Lord has commanded him to be commander over His people..."* Can there be any greater decree over ones life than to have God proclaim one as an individual after His own heart? I think not. David's heart pleased the Lord. He was by no means a perfect man, but God knew his burning love and passion for Him!

God was saying to Jeremiah that there will not just be a man (or one individual), but there will be a company of shepherds (authentic spiritual fathers and mothers), after his own heart, which would guide and feed God's people.

True shepherds are able to feed God's flock with *knowledge and understanding* because they have feasted on the very heart of God. They have treasured His love, His emotions, His dreams, His hopes, His will, His nature, His intent and His mercy. Like Jeremiah, they too will herald the call to backslidden Nations, calling them up out of their perversions and iniquities. They will cry aloud to those who have forgotten the Lord - Return to GOD – He is faithful and true!

These shepherds have known the love of Christ experientially as Paul writes, *"...to know the love of Christ which passes knowledge; that you may be filled with all the fullness of God.* (Ephesians 3:19) Experiential revelation surpasses knowledge.

Before Bren and I had children, we had the *knowledge* and counsel of friends and family, advising us that kids were going to change our entire lives. But the truth is, we had no idea as to the depths to which our lives would be changed. Children would bring an amazing new reality. So it is with experiential knowledge, it causes true understanding that changes us, conforming us into His image. One of my mentors would always say, *"When you say you know, when you don't know – you'll never know."* I love that! And it's loaded with such rich truth. The Holy Spirit is fully committed to your journey to make truth known experientially in the core of your being. Your cry must be, *"God, I want to know!"*

God patiently builds and grooms spiritual fathers and mothers experientially, through the journey and process of faith. There are no shortcuts. It is through His refining fire, in both valleys and mountaintops, that revelation and wisdom are imparted. When God's heart has become your sole obsession, you will feed God's flock with true knowledge and understanding.

As many are becoming true shepherds *after His own heart,* The Spirit of God is actively removing and dealing with hirelings and false shepherds that have troubled our Nation and have grossly mis-represented the character and nature of God. Isaiah called them, *greedy dogs!*

Isaiah 56:11 | NKJV
"Yes, they are greedy dogs which never have enough. And they are shepherds who cannot understand; they all look to their own way, every one for his own gain, from his own territory."

God's true shepherds, His spiritual fathers and mothers do not seek their own. Their desire is for the greater good of their spiritual sons and daughters. Within their hearts lay the treasures for future generations!

A few months after Jim prophesied over me, I was in the Word one morning when God ambushed me with this scripture from David's psalm. When I saw David's cry for the generations my heart was penetrated with revelation – I am called to generations! I believe you are too!

Contending For Generations

Psalm 71:17 &18 | NKJV
*"O God, You have taught me **from my youth**; And to this day **I declare Your wondrous works.** Now also when I am old and grayheaded, O God, do not forsake me, **Until I declare Your strength to this genera-***

117

tion, Your power to everyone who is to come."

God loves generations! From this Psalm, I can feel the burning desire of David as he contemplated the significance of passing the burning torch to those among him and those who were *yet to come*. God had set generational legacy within him, and he kept telling the stories of his journey with God to reveal God's faithfulness, strength and power. There is great power in the telling! You must never stop telling what God has done in you and through you. It's the testimony of Jesus. (Revelation 19:10)

It's a beautiful thing when God opens our hearts and hands to impart to others. David's Psalm expanded my heart with flaming passion and set my spiritual compass for living, thinking and planning generationally. It was the key that would keep my heart in cadence with His rhythmic guidance. I have been fully persuaded that I am to march to the beat of His drum at any cost. I made my commitments young in life to invest in people and give what I could for their greater good. Jesus said, *freely you have received, freely give.*

Psalm 71:17 &18 | NKJV
*"O God, You have taught me from my youth; And to this day I declare Your wondrous works. Now also when I am old and grayheaded, O God, do not forsake me, **Until I declare Your strength to this generation, Your power to everyone who is yet to come."***

Notice David's words, *"Oh God, you have taught me from my youth and to this day I declare your wonderful works..."* David kept the power of his testimony fresh, by telling the exploits of how God moved faithfully throughout his journey in trials and in triumph over and over again. Can you image sitting with David and hearing him tell the story of the prophet Samuel arriving at his house and pouring the fragrant anointing oil over his head in the presence of his family that day? Can you imagine David telling you about the bear and lion he killed when protecting the sheep? Can you imagine David sharing what it was like walking out on the battlefield that day and running to kill the warring champion, Goliath - cutting off His head! How about running for his life fr om Saul and overcoming attacks, defamation, rejection, loneliness and pain? How about the day the ark of His Presence arrived back in Jerusalem and the party that broke out in honor of The God of wonders? Throughout his life, David kept recalling the goodness and faithfulness of God. With every epic battle and every extraordinary victory – through them - he testified of God's grace, empowering the next generation to never quit, never give up, keep the fire burning - no matter what adversity comes!

God loves the generations!

Psalm 145:4-7 & 11-14 | NKJV

*"One generation shall praise Your works to another, And shall **declare Your mighty acts**. I will meditate **on the glorious splendor of Your majesty**, And on Your **wondrous works**. Men shall **speak of the might of Your awesome acts**, And I will declare **Your greatness**. They shall utter the memory of **Your great goodness**, And shall **sing of Your righteousness**....They shall **speak of the glory of Your kingdom**, And **talk of Your power**,To make known to the sons of men His mighty acts, And the **glorious majesty of His kingdom**. Your kingdom is an everlasting kingdom, And Your dominion endures throughout all generations."*

Isn't that awesome! David's heart cry was to release a legacy, through the generations, of the glory, power and wonder of God! Though he was not perfect, David lived thoughtfully and skillfully that he might bless the generations that were yet to come. God would use his life, wasting nothing – his victories, his failures, his dreams and desire to be a launching pad for generational blessing, so great that even Jesus Himself would sit upon the throne of David! Amazing!

Daniel 4:3 | NASB

"How great are His signs, And how mighty His wonders! His kingdom is an everlasting kingdom, And His dominion is from generation to generation."

King Hezekiah

Hezekiah was a strong and righteous king to Israel but he lacked the ability to contend for generational victory. In Isaiah 38, it reveals how the king became very sick. *"In those days Hezekiah was sick and near death. And Isaiah the prophet, the son of Amoz, went to him and said to him, "Thus says the Lord: 'Set your house in order, for you shall die and not live.'" Then Hezekiah turned his face toward the wall, and prayed to the Lord, and said, "Remember now, O Lord, I pray, how I have walked before You in truth and with a loyal heart, and have done what is good in Your sight." And Hezekiah wept bitterly. And the word of the Lord came to Isaiah, saying, "Go and tell Hezekiah, 'Thus says the Lord, the God of David your father: "I have heard your prayer, I have seen your tears; surely I will add to your days fifteen years. I will deliver you and this city from the hand of the king of Assyria, and I will defend this city."' And this is the sign to you from the Lord, that the Lord will do this thing which He has spoken: "Behold, I will bring the shadow on the sundial, which has gone down with the sun on the sundial of Ahaz, ten degrees backward." So the sun returned ten degrees on the dial by which it had gone down."*

The Prophet, Isaiah, came into the king's chambers and told him to get his house in order, because he was about to die. When Isaiah left, Hezekiah rolled over in his bed, weeping and crying out to the Lord God. His repentance and brokenness were so sincere that it moved God. Once again, at the Lord's direction, Isaiah turned around and went back to the king's chamber, saying to him: "God has heard your words and your cry. He has heard your repentance, Hezekiah and behold He's going to give you another 15 years."

It's fascinating, that later, in Isaiah 39, Hezekiah would make the dreadful decision to show his enemies his treasuries. The consequences would be heavy.

Then Isaiah said to Hezekiah, "Hear the word of the Lord of hosts: 'Behold, the days are coming when all that is in your house, and what your fathers have accumulated until this day, shall be carried to Babylon; nothing shall be left,' says the Lord. 'And they shall take away some of your sons who will descend from you, whom you will beget; and they shall be eunuchs in the palace of the king of Babylon.'" Don't miss this response!

*So Hezekiah said to Isaiah, "**The word of the Lord which you have spoken is good!**" For he said, "**At least there will be peace and truth*** *in my days*."

Perhaps our biblical emphasis and highlights have been short sight-ed, when we look at King Hezekiah. He's praised and celebrated for his repentance and tears, earning him the gift of 15 more years from The Lord. But I submit to you that Hezekiah was much like some of the ministries of today – shockingly self-absorbed! Upon hearing of the calamities, which would befall his children, why didn't Hezekiah tear his clothes open and fall to his knees? Why wouldn't he cry out with the same intensity and desperation for his children's breakthrough as he had for his own life? How was it enough for him to be settled with peace in his lifetime and not be moved to contend with unrelenting prayer to see war and affliction thwarted in his children's times? His response is utterly pathetic! He told Isaiah, *"The word which you have spoken is good."* Good? Really? Pretty shortsighted! God had just promised him 15 more years. Talk about mercy. After hearing that these calamities were to be released upon coming generations, due to his carelessness, he said, ***"At least there will be peace and truth*** *in my days*." Whoa!

I've grown weary of the preachers that are in love with the sound of their own voice. They're the sun in their own constellations. All they can see is their "day" - their ministries, their message, their church, their series, their…well, you get it! This has caused many abuses and casualties in the Body of Christ. The next generation is looking for authentic fathers and mothers to impart love, wisdom, life and anointing. They long to be fathered and empowered. Re-member, we need fathers, not just advisors. Advisors set codes, but fathers lay a clear path through examples of conduct. Fathers provide a burning and passionate example to follow. Fathers like the Apostle Paul can say, *"Follow me as I follow Christ."* If you are to father, you must pledge yourself to wholeheartedly pray, love, train, nurture and build those rising up, that they may be the un-quenchable arrows of fire shot throughout the earth, to release the gospel of glory. While we thank God for the present days of re-newal and revival, we must set our focus to the generations to come from faith to faith and glory to glory…*until the kingdoms of this world have become the kingdoms of our Lord!* (Rev 11:15)

David Prepared Generationally

When God told David that He would not let him build Him a House, David set a plan in motion for Solomon's day to make sure they would have all that they would need to build the Temple of The Lord.

David, this grand worshipper, was thinking and preparing generationally. I encourage you to read chapters 22, 28 & 29 of 1 Chronicles, and look at the work, planning and intention of David. He was thorough and abundant in preparations. Look at the details of gold, silver, bronze, iron (with no limit)...timber, stones and precious stones. Look at the spirit of excellence, seen in the raising up skilled workers of every kind. Why? Because he had a heart like God's, which was focused on building for those who were *yet to come*...so that a new generation could go further and higher into the glory of God!

Long before Martin Smith (lead singer of Delirious & worship leader) would pen the song *"His Fire Never Sleeps"*, David was working, planning and appointing certain Levites to minister before the ark of the Lord. They were precisely instructed to record (or bring to remembrance what God has done), to thank and to praise the Lord of Israel with psalteries, harps, cymbals, trumpets and songs continually (1 Chron. 16:4-6). David hired 4,000 Levite musicians and 288 Levites singers to minister to God (1 Chron. 25:7, Ps. 134-1-3) nonstop. That's a vision! And that's quite a worship staff!

The first psalm selection was a psalm of instruction, written and presented by David on that first day of his ministry. (1 Chron. 16:8-11; Ps. 105:1-4)

1 Chronicles 16:7-11 NKJV | *"On that day David first delivered this psalm into the hand of Asaph and his brethren, to thank the Lord: Oh, give thanks to the Lord! Call upon His name; Make known His deeds among the peoples! Sing to Him, sing psalms to Him; Talk of all His wondrous works! Glory in His holy name; Let the hearts of those rejoice who seek the Lord! Seek the Lord and His strength; Seek His face evermore!*

Are you feeling this? Generations burning for the heart of God!

Generations with unstoppable and unquenchable fire!

Generational Legacy

In this present move of God we are beginning to see the signs of generational impartation and the promise of kingdom legacy being expanded far and wide. Legacy is powerful - it's an endowment, a gift and commission - released with the hopeful expectation of increase from generation unto generation. Paul instructs his spiritual son Timothy, *"And the things that you have heard from me among many witnesses, **commit these to faithful men** who will be able to teach others also"* (2 Timothy 2:2)

There are those who are in training right now to become mighty spiritual fathers and mothers. Faithful sons and daughters become faithful fathers and mothers. Your allegiance must be fully unto The Lord, but your faithfulness to Him is also revealed in how you choose to serve and honor those He has brought into your life as fathers. One of the greatest privileges that we have is in choosing who we will follow, so choose wisely! Follow wisdom and character. Follow those who live in true humility and love. Do not be caught up in a leader's gifts and charisma. Watch their lives to see their consistent integrity. No leader is perfect or infallible. Look for the marks of a true father who will invest and speak truth into your life – the beautiful truth and the ugly truth. We need people in our lives who will do more than just comfort us in a crisis or compliment our strengths and gifts. We need fathers who will commit themselves to challenging us to grow and to change. This is necessary! We need fathers who will lovingly rebuke us in the healthiest way. The beautiful words of affirmation and empowerment are needed. So too, are the words of correction (hard sayings) and discipline.

You cannot be apostolic if you don't have the heart for sons and daughters. It's no secret that fathers today are abandoning their wives, children and responsibilities. It's a tragedy. Sadly, it's a picture of the spiritual condition of our world, as we see these same patterns of abandonment taking place in ministry. Presently, around 1500+ pastors quit the ministry each month. This is so alarming! Without a doubt, ministry is tough. After more than 20+ years of full-time ministry, I understand the challenges and the enormous load of responsibility that comes with leadership and becoming a father.

Spiritual fathers and mothers bring rich perspective, wise counsel and protection to our relationship with God. Their training, instruction, wisdom, covering, accountability and transparent lives are to be treasured. Having spiritual fathers and mothers help protect and safeguard the path and vision for your lives. They empower your God-given destiny and dream, regardless of weather it's to be a minister, a baseball coach, an actor, an artist a senator or an entrepreneur. Spiritual fathers provide a safe and nurturing environment to grow and also help us to identify spiritual gifts. Spiritual maturity is vital in all of our lives, and spiritual fathers will put an appropriate demand on us to grow from adolescence into adulthood. *"When I was a child, I spoke as a child, I understood as a child, I thought as a child; but when I became a man, I put away childish things."* (1 Corinthians 13:11) For many, they remain stuck in a perpetual place of immaturity, because they lack the nurture and sound admonition of seasoned fathers and mothers. Spiritual fathers model a standard of excellence and call forth that spirit of excellence in their sons and daughters.

Teachers instruct, but fathers love and build up. Teachers instruct but fathers impart. I am deeply grateful to the amazing fathers and mothers that the Lord has brought throughout my life, to help shape and develop me. I'm additionally thankful that they didn't ignore my mistakes but gracefully corrected me and pointed me forward. While so many leaders in our generation are waffling and wavering in a cesspool of social trends and compromise, I'm thankful for the fathers and leaders in my life who have kept burning faith, maintained integrity and have remained faithful on *the ancient path – the tried and true road.* (Jeremiah 6:16)

You need spiritual fathers and mothers in your life. It is imperative that you pray and seek to establish relationships (real kingdom connections) that will enhance and lift your spiritual trajectory and maturity. The passion of The Spirit is the return of apostolic fathers towards sons and daughters and sons and daughters toward fathers. (Malachi 4:6) Malachi's prophetic word is a beautiful picture of the generations from the youngest, to the most seasoned, working together to advance the kingdom of God!

To father the fire and perpetuate the kingdom's legacy, we must raise spiritual sons and daughters that have learned the secret of a saturated lifestyle in His Presence. Our aim must be to bring them to a place of character, where as mature sons and daughters, they carry the government of God. Only mature sons and daughters, who are discipled by godly fathers and mothers will be able to rule with nobility in the high places of cultural influence. We must create an atmosphere where it's the norm to linger before the Lord in prayer, and gaze upon His wonder and glory. You must father sons and daughters through example, so that their first and greatest ministry is unto the Lord. It's not *people* first. It's *Father* first. Lead them to cultivate a sacred lifestyle of encounter in the riches of the Word and with The Holy Spirit, through prayer, worship and fasting. Empower them to be courageous and brave, living as a nonconformist to the spirit of the Age. (Romans 12:2) Invest time, revelation and life experiences into their development. Our greatest legacy is not what we leave *for* people, but what you leave *within* them. Invest! Live an uncompromising and consecrated life before them. Let our testimony be a standard, witnessing God's empowerment and grace to a surrendered life.

God must be represented by those who are not bound by time. A spiritual father and mother are a timeless people who understand that their sacrifices, obedience, honor, joy, and life contributions are going to impart into a generation that perhaps even isn't born yet. Ecclesiastes 3:11 says, *"He has made everything beautiful in its time. Also He has put eternity in their hearts, except that no one can find out the work that God does from beginning to end."* We must understand that the eternity which has been set in our hearts, will not be completely unfolded and revealed in our lifetime, but will find its fullness in generational legacy.

I want to encourage you to make a personal commitment to serve, build and foster relationships that will perpetuate the kingdom of God. Make it your aim to live and plan skillfully to invest and empower young men and women. We need each other and we need mature and courageous leaders for the hour ahead of us. We are dependent upon one another. Together we can overcome the orphan and independent spirit that has plagued the Body of Christ for far too long. Remember, there are those who are in training right now to become mighty spiritual fathers and mothers. Faithful sons and daughters become faithful fathers and mothers.

Let me close this chapter with a beautiful testimony of God's passions for the generational blessing and inheritance.

Prophetic Justice

One night while ministering in a church in Indianapolis, we were hosting a prayer line for people with specific needs for healing. The altars were filled with several hundred individuals. After praying for a couple, I went back up on stage to make sure the ministry team wasn't missing any. I noticed an older lady was slowly making her way up to the front of the church and get into line. As I approached, I heard the Holy Spirit say the word – *Sonnet*. That may not mean anything to you, but I knew what a sonnet was. A sonnet is a particular poetic form or structure that originated in Italy, but became extremely popular through the poet and playwright William Shakespeare. A sonnet's main distinction is its pattern and structure that carries just 14 lines. The Holy Spirit highlighted 14 lines to me. I believe God has good things to say to people. He loves when we partner with Him to be a conduit of life in speaking His promises, desires and will to others. The Holy Spirit knows our language. He knows how to speak to us and draw from our *database* and life experiences. He is able to give us prophetic keys, enabling us to release life and healing to others.

I waited upon the Lord for a moment longer, and he directed my thoughts to **Psalm 16:5&6,** *"O Lord, You are the portion of my inheritance and my cup; You maintain my lot. **The lines** have fallen to me in pleasant places; Yes, I have a good inheritance."* Lines in scripture give a picture of inheritance, posterity and generations. I believed The Lord was showing me something profound, but honestly it took some courage and faith (spelled – R.I.S.K) to give this word. I committed myself and said to her, *"You have 14 grandchildren and* *you are not to worry as the Lord shows me every one of them will be saved and brought into the kingdom. This is your inheritance and portion!"*

The woman burst into tears and began to celebrate ecstatically, giving praises to the Lord! The Pastor asked me, *"Do you know this woman and her family?"* I didn't, and was clearly nervous about what I had just shared. I think the Pastor was too. But the woman testified that she indeed had 14 grandchildren. They were the very reason she came forward to have prayer. She didn't realize that the prayer line was for healing. Frankly it didn't matter. God wanted to reward her years of prayer and intercession for her family. God has generations on his mind!

In, Acts 16:31 it says to, *"Believe on the Lord Jesus Christ, and you will be saved, you and your household."* I felt usually stirred to include this testimony in this book. I believe it will serve those who are interceding right now, that their families (generations) will come into the kingdom! In Revelation 19:11, it says, *"...the testimony of Jesus is the spirit of prophecy."* This means that a testimony of what God has done, reveals what is available and accessible once again, in the present. When the hearing of a testimony goes forth, it brings faith into the present for the same miracle to be given again. God is no respecter of persons. What He has done for one, He can do for another...when they believe!

CHAPTER FIVE

TO THE OVERCOMERS

Overcome: to conquer, to prevail over; surmount, to ascend to the top, to overpower, to establish right.

I have dedicated this book to the new breed of emerging pioneers, revivalists and firebrands who are braving and overcoming every adversity to bring the Gospel of the Kingdom to the Nations. Without a doubt, the battles and conflicts that we are facing in our times are epic to say the least. We find ourselves living in the most peculiar and perilous times. The Apostle Paul's letter to his spiritual son, Timothy, is a letter to our generation as well. Listen to how he describes mankind in these last days.

2 Timothy 3:1-17 | NKJV

*"But know this, that in the last days perilous times will come: **For men will be lovers of themselves, lovers of money, boasters, proud, blasphemers, disobedient to parents, unthankful, unholy, unloving, unforgiving, slanderers, without self-control, brutal, despisers of good, traitors, headstrong, haughty, lovers of pleasure rather than lovers of God, having a form of godliness but denying its power. And from such people turn away...** so do these also resist the truth: men of corrupt minds, disapproved concerning the faith;*

but they will progress no further, for their folly will be manifest to all, as theirs also was."

This is the world that we presently live in, and it has become a very dark place. Our Nation has been pillaged and rampaged by vile sins and godlessness. I hope you didn't gloss over those words too quickly..."*proud, blasphemers, without self-control, brutal, despisers of good, traitors...haughty, unloving, slanderers, men of corrupt minds...*" The carnage and corruption of our generation is like a thick lingering stench, pervading the atmosphere. There is an unmistakably gross and deep darkness upon society in this hour, as *"the god of this age has blinded those who do not believe, lest the light of the gospel of the glory of Christ, who is the image of God, should shine on them."* (2 Corinthians 4:4) You have been called to prevail and ascend in this hour!

I suspect that some of you reading this book are presently in the ministry or in preparation to enter it, or perhaps you are looking for a way to get out of it. Be encouraged, the storms and battles you have waged this far will not go to waste! I want to remind you that God is building you. He is patiently sculpting and fashioning you into an instrument of healing and restoration, right now! What God is building will endure and be established. You may be weary right now in the journey. All of us have trudged through darkness. But you must never give up! Refuse to quit! You must overcome every obstacle and every snare of the wicked one. Your victory has been won in Christ, but you must remain steadfast in your vision and focus now. You *will* overcome discouragement and rejection. You *will* overcome confusion and the personal inner contradictions of your faith. You were born to overcome! The disorientation you have suffered must cause you to rely fully upon His strength and not your own. Sin will not prevail or have dominion over you. The demonic strategies of witchcraft and confusion will not win. You will not be overcome with evil... *"but you will overcome evil with good."* (Romans 12:21)

Some of you have endured considerable amounts of rejection and misunderstanding in your faith journey. Part of your training and building is learning to forgive those who have persecuted, you just as our Lord did. If we are going to walk in the Spirit and demonstrate authentic spiritual authority, we must overcome rejection. To walk in true spiritual authority we must become a man or a woman in whom, *"the love of Christ controls us"* (2 Corinthians 5:14). There can be no desire for self-preservation or self-promotion in this hour. We must simply desire only to fulfill our personal mission and assignment. Many have shipwrecked their ministries because they tried to run in a lane that they had no authorization and grace from Heaven in which to run. Paul made it clear we must not act in presumption - to go beyond our sphere of authority, appointed by the Lord (2 Corinthians 10:14-16). Stay true to what The Father has appointed you to accomplish, and be sure to consciously avoid going beyond that sphere. A police officer in Chicago has no authority in Dallas and we do not have spiritual authority beyond the realm of our God given assignment. The grace of God will establish you and His kingdom in the places you are called to serve.

Many have endured the onslaught of counterfeit authority in the church. Many weak and insecure leaders have wounded countless lives in their effort to control, out of territorial preservation. It is no secret that the Church can be a messy place. Sometimes the wounds afflicted within the family are the hardest to endure and withstand, but nonetheless, we must overcome them. Love always prevails! Jesus said, *"Bless those who curse you, and pray for those who spitefully use you."* (Matthew 5:44)

The Apostle Paul prayed in Philippians 1:9, *"And this I pray, that your love may abound still more and more in knowledge and all discernment..."* Notice that the foundation of true discernment is God's love. How have we missed this? Abounding love is the cornerstone of the Kingdom of God. Without being able to see with the eyes of love, our vision will be far from accurate and most certainly, not a heavenly perspective. Most of what is considered "discernment" in the church is really nothing more that *suspicion*. I believe it was Frances Frangipane who said: *"False discernment is based on mistrust, suspicion and fear. False discernment is always quick to anger, slow to hear and quick to speak."* To abound in love must be our devotion!

You were born to overcome. In your quest, it is absolutely imperative that you overcome the fear of man. I remember vividly when I was praying about moving to Florida years ago to pioneer a new church. The Lord spoke to me late one night in prayer and said: *"I'm not sending you there to be respectable, but I'm sending you there to be responsible for the spiritual destiny of that region."* This word held me together and caused me to stand victoriously through demonic attacks upon myself, my family and all those who yoked themselves to us, as we prepared the way of the Lord in a region.

Many long to have a "respectable" ministry. They long for their place of notoriety amongst the so-called influencers – the "movers" and "shakers" of their communities. That's not where authority is found. I've seen too many good leaders waste their time and energy courting all the wrong people in their cities. The problem? They have a fear of man. True spiritual authority is found on your knees, ministering before The King, and letting Him lay His heart upon you. This is our dilemma today. Men don't kneel. They plan, they strategize and they coerce through manipulation, looking to rub shoulders with all the wrong people. Is life lived for the approval of man or to please Him? Fear man?! No! My vows are unto Him and I plan to keep them.

King Saul's life is a tragic lesson of the falling into the fear of man. His commission from God was authentic, yet he fell into this snare that utterly perverted his authority and leadership. His fear grew and manifested full on into witchcraft, which ultimately caused him to be led about by murdering spirits. The story of King Saul and King David is an honest and epic unfolding that parallels our present times. Like David, we too must walk in wisdom to overcome the enemy by giving no place to him, by not retaliating against carnal and misguided leadership, but patiently letting God raise us up in due season.

You were born to overcome. Revivalist Smith Wigglesworth said: *"Great faith is the product of great fights. Great testimonies are the outcome of great tests. Great triumphs only come out of great trials."* You may have experienced temporary setbacks - even having been sabotaged by the enemy. Be encouraged, God will bring you into the place of ultimate victory. Remember the Apostle Paul's words, *" We are hard-pressed on every side, yet not crushed; we are perplexed, but not in despair; persecuted, but not forsaken; struck down, but not destroyed..."* (2 Corinthians 4:8&9) You are an overcomer!

Paul's perspective is much different from most followers of Christ. When he writes about the persecution and afflictions which came against him at Antioch, Iconium and Lystra, he audaciously declares: ***"And out of them all the Lord delivered me. Yes, and all who desire to live godly in Christ Jesus will suffer persecution."*** (2 Timothy 3:11&12) Do you remember what happened to Paul in these cities? He was imprisoned, stoned, beaten by raging mobs with rods, threatened and endangered by false brothers. When he was stoned in Lystra, it was so brutal, they supposed he was dead - leaving his body to rot. Yet Paul said that out of all the persecution, the Lord *"delivered"* him. What a perspective! He was crushed but not destroyed!

Again, Paul said, *"the Lord delivered him out of them all."* Thankfully, Paul was not some weak anemic Christian, who couldn't recognize victory in the face of affliction. Sadly, many believers today are quick to question the authenticity of God's will, because they encounter minor difficulties or challenges. We must remember that we too *"must endure hardship as a good soldier of Christ."* (2 Timothy 2:3) You were born to overcome!

1 Corinthians 15:57 | NASB
"But thanks be to God, who gives us the victory through our Lord Jesus Christ."

Romans 8:37 | AMP
"Yet amid all these things we are more than conquerors and gain a surpassing victory through Him Who loved us."

Overcoming the Contradictions

Romans 5:1-5 | NKJV

"Therefore, having been justified by faith, we have peace with God through our Lord Jesus Christ, through whom also we have access by faith into this grace in which we stand, and rejoice in hope of the glory of God. And not only that, but we also glory in tribulations, knowing that tribulation produces perseverance; and perseverance, character; and character, hope. Now hope does not disappoint, because the love of God has been poured out in our hearts by the Holy Spirit who was given to us."

What a perspective! Glory in tribulations...tribulations producing perseverance...perseverance bringing forth character. In Luke 22, Jesus is teaching his disciples how authority is demonstrated in the kingdom of God. In the midst of shaping these truths within their hearts, he makes this amazing statement: *"But you are those who have continued with Me in My trials. And I bestow a kingdom, just as My Father bestowed one upon Me, that you may eat and drink at My table in the kingdom, and sit down on thrones judging the twelve tribes of Israel."* (Luke 22:28-30)

This is no small conversation. It's interesting that the disciples had been arguing about which one of them should really be considered the greatest among them. Can you imagine? Yet, Jesus drops a bombshell on them. He's bestowing an everlasting kingdom on them that cannot be shaken. He is making a place of privilege and honor to eat at His table. He is establishing a place of authority and ruling upon thrones. However, notice these words, *"you have continued with Me in My trials"*. They had remained faithful to Jesus. They stood with Him, even though He was opposed and reviled. In essence, they were in training to learn how to overcome through the contradictions.

Luke 12:32 | KJV

"Do not fear, little flock, for it is your Father's good pleasure to give you the kingdom."

Many of you have received notable promises and remarkable words from the Lord, concerning your calling and purpose. Did you

134

notice that once these words were revealed in your life that seemingly every potential contradiction moved swiftly against you? Don't be naive. The truth is; the Word and will of God spoken over us brings us to a place of real conflict. Jesus told us in Mark, chapter four, that Satan comes immediately to try and steal the Word sown, lest it begin to work and produce. Within the place of conflict and resistance, we discover the superior power and glory of His word, working in our lives. The enemy opposes the Word with every possible contradiction in his arsenal of lies. But as you believe, the Word will be established in you, gaining power and endurance, enabling you to overcome. With every contradiction, remember that the voice you believe will determine the future you experience.

James 1:1-8 & 12 | NKJV

*"My brethren, **count it all joy when you fall into various trials**, knowing that the testing of your faith produces patience. But let patience have its perfect work, that you may be perfect and complete, lacking nothing. If any of you lacks wisdom, let him ask of God, who gives to all liberally and without reproach, and it will be given to him. **But let him ask in faith**, with no doubting, for he who doubts is like a wave of the sea driven and tossed by the wind.*

*For let not that man suppose that he will receive anything from the Lord; he is a **double-minded man, unstable in all his ways.**"*

*"**Blessed is the man who endures temptation; for when he has been approved, he will receive the crown of life which the Lord has promised to those who love Him.**"*

Trials are singular circumstances which sifts out double-mindedness. To be single minded is to be of the mind of faith. Faith is simply to trust and believe God at all times. Joseph's life is an epic unfolding, demonstrating how one might overcome the contradictions of trials. He received dreams of great honor, ruling, authority and privilege…yet through the agony of rejection, betrayal by his own family, defamation, being falsely accused and forgotten…he endured and arrived at the destination and purpose and saw His dreams fulfilled. He overcame, and learned the secret of ruling in the midst of his enemies.

135

You were born to overcome. In these trials and contradictions that you presently face, you must draw healing, hope and supernatural nourishment from the Presence of God. It is here that His friendship becomes your home and safe place. He is building you to receive His everlasting kingdom. You have suffered indescribable things along the journey - things that have surprised you and left you bewildered. God is greater than any setback! He will heal you from the arrows of betrayal. He will unravel the twisted and tied up memories from the cruel intentions of men. He will soothe your soul from life's damage and silence the voices of mockery. He will deflect the fiery darts with His shield of love. I know this, because I too have experienced them. But I can tell you, with full assurance, that you will overcome! Yes, *He who has promised is faithful!* His fire will energize and fuel your dreams afresh.

Believers can gain access to a supernatural strength from the Presence of The Lord. They need only take the depths of the loss and pain they have experienced to the feet of Jesus. Then, allow the Holy Spirit to transform them into life-giving conduits, despite their losses. Spirit led people use life's worst moments to make themselves even better. They are unstoppable because of Who abides within!

Our Father believes in you, and you must believe in His perfect work in you and through you. Whatever Jesus has called you to do, you must not procrastinate, hesitate or deviate from that mandate. Your potential is limitless in Him. But you must overcome!

Overcoming Sin & Compromise

"Do not love the world or the things in the world. If anyone loves the world, the love of the Father is not in him. For all that is in the world—the lust of the flesh, the lust of the eyes, and the pride of life—is not of the Father but is of the world. And the world is passing away, and the lust of it; but he who does the will of God abides forever."
1 John 2:15-17 | NKJV

"I know your works, that you are neither cold nor hot. I could wish you

were cold or hot. So then, because you are lukewarm, and neither cold nor hot, I will vomit you out of My mouth. Because you say, 'I am rich, have become wealthy, and have need of nothing' – and do not know that you are wretched, miserable, poor, blind, and naked – I counsel you to buy from Me gold refined in the fire, that you may be rich; and white garments, that you may be clothed, that the shame of your nakedness may not be revealed; and anoint your eyes with eye salve, that you may see. As many as I love, I rebuke and chasten. Therefore be zealous and repent. Behold, I stand at the door and knock. If anyone hears My voice and opens the door, I will come in to him and dine with him, and he with Me. **To him who overcomes I will grant to sit with Me on My throne, as I also overcame and sat down with My Father on His throne."**
Revelation 3:15-21 | NKJV

You were born to overcome sin and compromise – to live victoriously. We find ourselves in the midst of disturbing times, as our Nation is growing morally darker. The Church is suffering humiliation and shame, as story after story of leaders' moral compromises wreak havoc on the Body. The world is fully aware of the Church's abuse of authority and it's lack of accountability. It is detested for its hypocrisy. We're in trouble, and the reproach is warranted. Believers are masking their inner wounds and conflicts to walk in purity and with integrity before the Lord. God is calling for a radical change! Sin has an ultimate remedy – The Cross!

The promise given by Jesus to the overcomer is one of incomprehensible grace. It's unfathomable that Almighty God would give such a privilege as to sit with Him upon His throne! The good news is – it is possible to overcome! To overcome the sin and the lusts of this world, we must first receive the truth that Jesus has crushed the power of sin and has delivered you and me from its dominion.

Colossians 1:13-14 | NKJV
"He has delivered us from the power of darkness and conveyed us into the kingdom of the Son of His love, in whom we have re-demption through His blood, the forgiveness of sins."

This has been accomplished! He has conveyed (carried, lifted, transported, imparted, transferred) you and me up from the power of darkness and into His kingdom of love. His blood paid in full our penalty of sin and imparted forgiveness. The crushing blow to sin came at the Cross, where He died, and we died with Him!

Romans 6:1-14 | NKJV

"What shall we say then? Shall we continue in sin that grace may abound? Certainly not! How shall we who died to sin live any longer in it? Or do you not know that as many of us as were baptized into Christ Jesus were baptized into His death? Therefore we were buried with Him through baptism into death, that just as Christ was raised from the dead by the glory of the Father, even so we also should walk in newness of life."

"For if we have been united together in the likeness of His death, certainly we also shall be in the likeness of His resurrection, knowing this, that our old man was crucified with Him, that the body of sin might be done away with, that we should no longer be slaves of sin. For he who has died has been freed from sin. Now if we died with Christ, we believe that we shall also live with Him, knowing that Christ, having been raised from the dead, dies no more. Death no longer has dominion over Him. For the death that He died, He died to sin once for all; but the life that He lives, He lives to God. Likewise you also, reckon yourselves to be dead indeed to sin, but alive to God in Christ Jesus our Lord."

Paul is not saying that the only way to be free from sin is to die. Where's the hope in that belief? Death is surely not our deliverance from sin. He is clearly revealing that the victory over sin was provided at the Cross - when we were crucified with Christ. And because we died with Him, we have been made free from sin!

So many men and women, whom I have pastored throughout the years, have suffered from these lies, *"I'll never be able to find freedom from this...it's just going to remain part of my life until I die."* Friends, that's a lie, and this lie that has held so many in perpetual bondage must be exposed! If that were true, then the Cross holds no power.

Don't be *destroyed because of a lack of knowledge* (Hosea 4:6). The Cross is the ultimate victory over sin! The first step to victory is to understand that in Christ, freedom has *already* been won. The man or woman who has died with Christ has been freed from sin. Jesus died so that His victory could be ours in every area of our lives. His passion is that your soul is healed...your memory and imagination are made new...your thoughts are filled with life and peace. This is our inheritance from The Savior!

Because you have become His dwelling place - literally, the ark of His glory - you are not subject to the bullying and slavery of lust and sin. You are now the *slave unto righteousness* – qualified and justified by His blood in right standing with The Father. The power of your yielded and surrendered will to the Holy Spirit's authority will ensure your victory every time. He took residence within us, unwilling to share us with another.

Romans 6:12-14 | NKJV
" Therefore do not let sin reign in your mortal body, that you should obey it in its lusts. And do not present your members as instruments of unrighteousness to sin, but present yourselves to God as being alive from the dead, and your members as instruments of righteousness to God. For sin shall not have dominion over you, for you are not under law but under grace."

You and I are enveloped in His beautiful and amazing grace. Grace is His empowering Presence, which enables us to become the person that He sees when He looks at us. Grace in no way overlooks or excuses sin. It empowers righteousness in us, to please God and live in union with our Father. It is true that grace is God's loving-kindness and unmerited favor. Yet grace also forgives and empowers the believer from within, so that he or she may live in victory over sin and defilement.

Titus 2:11-14 | NKJV
"For the grace of God that brings salvation has appeared to all men, teaching us that, denying ungodliness and worldly lusts, we should live soberly, righteously, and godly in the present age, look-

*ing for the blessed hope and glorious appearing of our great God and Savior Jesus Christ, who gave Himself for us, **that He might redeem us from every lawless deed and purify for Himself His own special people, zealous for good works."***

Purity, integrity and holiness are not "old fashioned". Integrity and example matters greatly. The world is changed by your example. Your character is your life's unending message of hope to the world. When Paul wrote Timothy, he reminded him, *"Let no one despise your youth, but be an example to the believers in word, in conduct, in love, in spirit, in faith, in purity"*. (1 Timothy 4:12) Our character and integrity reveal the blooming person within. To grow and steward integrity, it is vital that you secure your personal vows and convictions unto The Lord and give no place for compromise.

Accountability starts with you. Leadership begins with leading yourself. You must practice and activate truth with yourself first. It is lofty and immature not to recognize that there is no exemption from sexual temptation. One of the keys to maintaining consistent victory is to fearlessly give oneself to men or women of uncommon character, who will guard and foster transparency and humility. While many are working hard to manage their image, God is calling us to manage our integrity and character. It is time for you to place the highest value in building your community of covenant keeping friends. Perhaps God will use you to pioneer a team of winners that burn zealously for holiness. Together we can prevail triumphantly!

With unbroken focus, we must aim our lives for integrity and purity. Refuse to be the man or woman who lives the aimless life obeying carnal impulses and urges. In aiming for holiness, you will conquer all degrading and distracting desires by the power of The Spirit. Never re-embrace sin's temporal pleasures from the past. Paul told Timothy, *"Retain the standard of sound words which you have heard from me, in the faith and love which are in Christ Jesus. Guard, through the Holy Spirit who dwells in us, the treasure which has been entrusted to you."* (2 Timothy 1:13-14 NASB) Make no mistake; Satan would love nothing more than to steal your treasure and that is why you must be vigilant to guard it!

A man or a woman who walks in friendship and reverential fear of the Lord will overcome sin. Remember, we are the friends of God! Our friendship with God, however, is proven by our faithfulness - not taking His friendship for granted. I love the Lord, but also fear Him and worship Him. The person who honors and fears the Lord will actually deflect sin!

"The friendship of the Lord is for
those who fear Him."
Psalm 24:14 | NRSV

"Fear-of God deflects evil"
Proverbs 16:6b | MSG

Repentance is a sacred and beautiful gift from God. He is the One who makes all things new. Forgiveness is received by those who repent of their sins. You may have failed the Lord in the past, but your future can be without blemish, if you will honestly deal with your soul and make room for the Holy Spirit to cleanse your heart with His all-consuming fire. Is God dealing with issues and areas of your life, ministry or values that are out of alignment? Spiritual refreshment and restoration flows to a humble and repentant heart.

An overcomer is one who diligently and continually puts his or her faith in Jesus Christ! The time is urgent. The hope for America is those burning firebrand believers and leaders, who are living in integrity and holiness. God is raising and restoring a new breed of pioneers, a true remnant company, who will live an irreproachable life and make no provisions for the flesh! You were born to overcome! Victory is branded upon your heart and soul!

2 Corinthians 7:1 | NKJV
"Therefore, having these promises, beloved, let us cleanse ourselves from all filthiness of the flesh and spirit, perfecting holiness in the fear of God."

Romans 13:11-14 | NKJV
"And do this, knowing the time, that now it is high time to awake

out of sleep; for now our salvation is nearer than when we first believed. The night is far spent, the day is at hand. Therefore let us cast off the works of darkness, and let us put on the armor of light. Let us walk properly, as in the day, not in revelry and drunkenness, not in lewdness and lust, not in strife and envy. But put on the Lord Jesus Christ, and make no provision for the flesh, to fulfill its lusts."

CHAPTER SIX

CALLING ALL REFORMERS!

Reformation means to align, reconstitute, to level & balance. It's repairing and restoring what has been broken and corrupted. Reformation is divine order and alignment with The King's purpose and design.

He was only eight years of age, when Prince Josiah was crowned King and began his reign over Judah. He is one of the most noble and righteous kings in all of Israel's history. He had an amazing burning heart for God. The Scriptures reveal that the greatest revival and reformation in all of Israel's history came under the leadership of King Josiah.

Generations after King David, "the giant killer", had passed on, the nation of Israel was lost in darkness. Tragically, the kings of the line of David forsook The Almighty God who had performed so many wonders and miracles for their people - delivering them from their enemies. These kings were some of the most wicked, evil, demonic, and violent kings to ever rule a nation on the Earth. For 300 years the temple of God was desecrated by its own kings and people. The sacred scriptures were outlawed and destroyed. The "glory days" of Solomon's Temple were long forgotten. Now Israel's Temple was nothing more than a museum of an ancient religion, long past. Josiah's father, King Amon, had just been assassinated and Israel was shrouded in gross darkness.

Noting how the Scriptures had been outlawed and destroyed for some 300 years, try to imagine what the church in America would look like without the Bible for that same period of time. I know, it's a terrifying thought! Can you imagine the heresy, the idolatry, false teaching, false doctrine and false prophets? Can you imagine the weird and bizarre practices that would be going on in the church without the Scriptures? We presently have serious trouble as it is *with* the Scriptures.

Tragically, some pastors and leaders throughout our Nation have been seduced into espousing false teachings, heresies and doctrines of devils. These include such falsities as: The Gospel of Inclusion, Deification of Man, Universal Reconciliation, "Chrislam" (the belief that Christians and Muslims serve the same God) and Modern-Grace. Like falling dominoes, pastors and other church leaders are leading the sheep into compromise with secular society and the pressure to universal tolerance. Today, these puppets of Satan are challenging the validity of the Word of God and even preaching there is no such place as an eternal hell. Churches are embracing homosexuality and sexual sins as a part of an evolving culture and society. Many of these wayward leaders – rather deceivers - are *"coming out of the closet"* and unashamedly advocating their poisonous heresies. We are in trouble! My heart is fervently burning to sound the alarm! The ignorance in the body of Christ is astounding, and the lack of understanding of the Scriptures is overwhelming! Just as in Josiah's day, we need a revival and mass awakening of the WORD of GOD!

> *"Now the Spirit expressly says that in latter times some will depart from the faith, giving heed to deceiving spirits and doctrines of demons, speaking lies in hypocrisy, having their own conscience seared with a hot iron..."*
> **1 Timothy 4:1&2 | NKJV**

The Narrow Road & The Broad Road

After Jesus' unprecedented message from the "Sermon on the Mount" in Matthew Chapters 5&6, He discusses two different responses to those who profess to be loyal to Him and His Word. We see this distinction from which He calls - *the narrow way and the broad way.*

Jesus said: *"Enter by the narrow gate; for wide is the gate and broad is the way that leads to destruction, and there are many who go in by it. Because narrow is the gate and difficult is the way which leads to life, and there are few who find it. "Beware of false prophets, who come to you in sheep's clothing, but inwardly they are ravenous wolves. You will know them by their fruits. Do men gather grapes from thornbushes or figs from thistles? Even so, every good tree bears good fruit, but a bad tree bears bad fruit. A good tree cannot bear bad fruit, nor can a bad tree bear good fruit. Every tree that does not bear good fruit is cut down and thrown into the fire. Therefore by their fruits you will know them.*

"Not everyone who says to Me, 'Lord, Lord,' shall enter the kingdom of heaven, but he who does the will of My Father in heaven. Many will say to Me in that day, 'Lord, Lord, have we not prophesied in Your name, cast out demons in Your name, and done many wonders in Your name?' And then I will declare to them, 'I never knew you; depart from Me, you who practice lawlessness!' "Therefore whoever hears these sayings of Mine, and does them, I will liken him to a wise man who built his house on the rock: and the rain descended, the floods came, and the winds blew and beat on that house; and it did not fall, for it was founded on the rock. But everyone who hears these sayings of Mine, and does not do them, will be like a foolish man who built his house on the sand: and the rain descended, the floods came, and the winds blew and beat on that house; and it fell. And great was its fall."
Matthew 7:13-27 | NKJV

The distinction Jesus makes here is painfully clear. One had a true relationship with God, the other was deceived into believing he had a relationship with God, but didn't. Jesus tragically replies, *"I never knew you"*.

Real freedom and liberty is not liberty apart from Jesus' leadership and authority. Freedom in the kingdom of God is not a free-for-all. There is divine order and government in the kingdom of God. True liberty is liberation from sin, defilement and things that darken our hearts. There are a lot of people in the body of Christ who claim grace, yet desire "liberties" from Jesus' commands and restraints. They want His forgiveness, but they refuse to obey the call to responsibility and holiness. That's not a biblical Christianity! Jesus is making clear that there is a false road and true road - the broad way that leads to destruction or the narrow way that leads to life. He is not contrasting the Church and the world here in this message. He is speaking to those who profess loyalty, faithfulness and authenticity in their faith, but their self-deception has them headed for eternal destruction. It's remarkable the number of people who have grown up in church and have been effectively Christianized, professing to know God, but have never genuinely met Christ. It is terrifying to think that many souls could hear these words, *"Depart from Me, I never knew you."*

The narrow way must be the highest priority of your life - to know and love the heart of God. It is about true friendship and intimacy with the Lord. God knows those who have made Him the sole passion of their hearts, and those who just profess His name, but inwardly are not joined in relationship. The heart that walks the narrow way is fearfully aware of sin's defilement and it guards itself, so that it might be presented unto the Lord as a clean and honorable vessel. Such hearts are those which *"fear The Lord and depart from evil."* (Proverbs 3:7) The narrow road is the *only road* in New Testament Christianity. The travelers along the narrow way look for the grace that delivers them from sin and empowers them. *"For the **grace of God that brings salvation** has appeared to all men, **teaching us that, denying ungodliness and worldly lusts, we should live soberly, righteously, and godly in the present age...**"* (Titus 2:12) Those who travel the narrow road are those who **work out their salvation with fear and trembling; for it is God who works in you both to will and to do for His good pleasure.** *(Philippians 2:12&13)* The narrow and loyal followers of The Master are those with sincerity, who consecrate their hearts and yield their lives

148

unto The Lord's work within them, so that they may be holy and sanctified. Holiness is not old fashion, friend. The narrow way follower is not bound by restriction, but bound by love.

The broad road is a road of tolerance, compromise and has very few restrictions. It is a road of permissiveness in the grace of God. It's wide open for many opinions, ideologies and lifestyles. On the broad road, you can keep your carry-on luggage of immorality, a little drunkenness, some slander and gossip with a hint of defamation...a little porn and lust here and there with little regard for the warnings of The Holy Spirit or repentance. The travelers along the broad road are always looking for a *grace* that covers their indulgences and pleasures, because they believe God is aware of weakness, yet his grace pardons them. The preachers of the broad road use the Bible all the time for their indulgences, yet they bear no fruits of true repentance in denying the flesh and keeping to spiritual disciplines. Moses brought us the law; but Jesus came to bring **grace and truth.** (John 1:17) There's the beautiful truth and the ugly truth - remember, it's a two-edged sword. Make no mistake, grace is beautiful, but if you abuse its beauty with lawlessness, you're in danger of hell fire. Without truth, there is a distorted message, promoting a certain confidence, which allows people to continue in compromise. Jesus said their destruction will be more terrifying than they can ever imagine when they stand face to face with Him. This must not be your story!

Today we have *modern grace teachers* who tell us that we don't need to repent of sins, as we are under His grace. Do not be deceived, friend. Grace comes as a beautiful and marvelous gift from the heart of our Father, to those who repent of their sins and long to live in pure union with God's heart. (1 John 1:9) Grace will transform you. Grace is not an invitation to fall into sin. It's an invitation to fall in Love.

If you are going to live the true grace lifestyle, the abundant life that Christ gives, you must be sure that you deny fleshly lust. To be a disciple and authentic follower of Jesus, this is paramount. Jesus said: *"Strive to enter through the narrow gate, for many, I say to you, will seek to enter and will not be able."* Strive means to make every effort of commitment. Let me be clear, we do not strive to earn God's love or forgiveness. We don't pray and fast to motivate God to love us...of course not! Christianity is not a behavioral modification, self-improvement or sin management program. It's the indwelling of the Spirit of God that transforms a life from the inside out. His ministry is unparalleled! Grace is about covenant relationship. We strive to give meaningful effort to the relationship, just as a husband does in his marriage to his wife.

As a husband, I aim and strive to strengthen the commitment and devotion my wife and I have to one another, and our children. When someone makes no effort to invest in a relationship, love could be brought into question. Our *striving* is an expression of honor and devotion, making every effort to position our heart in alignment with Him - that His grace can empower us over sin. We must strive with zealous determination to deny sin at all times and *give no place for the devil* (Ephesians 4:27).

It is by no means a contradiction to strive courageously to enter the narrow gate, which Jesus said comes with *difficulty and challenge*, and to wear His yoke, which is easy and light. Jesus was warning His hearers of the yoke of the Pharisees, which was a burdensome and oppressive yoke of self-righteousness and legalistic law keeping. Many bible scholars have said that the Pharisees had added over 600 regulations, regarding what qualified as 'working' on the Sabbath. That is a heavy burden! The Lord's yoke is light and easy to carry, because it is the yoke of repentance and faith, followed by a singular commitment to honor Him. Frankly, the narrow road is hard on our flesh – to overcome and deny sin - as we take up our cross and die daily. The yoke of Jesus speaks of taking on lowliness of heart (true meekness). Jesus is inviting us into a lifestyle of dying to the things we must die to, so that we might experience His yoke of liberation.

This is the narrow way. It's not a popular message, but it's the only biblical message of true grace. Grace leads to real life and a vibrant heart. For those who *fear the Lord and depart from evil*, the promise remains true – *it will be health to your flesh and strength to your bones.* (Proverbs 3:7&8) Striving to fully honor Jesus will lead to the abundant life, eternal reward and true encounters with The Lord. This is the fruit of true love.

Philippians 3:12 | NKJV
"Not that I have already obtained all this, or have already arrived at my goal, But I am pressing on, striving to take hold of that for which Christ Jesus took hold of me."

As sons and daughters of God, it should be our daily aim and our lifelong pursuit to strive to honor the grace of our Father. Paul urged the church to *"aim for perfection"*. (2 Corinthians 13:11) Dear friend, in our pursuit, let us remember these urgent and passionate words from Paul: *"We then, as workers together with Him also plead with you not to receive the grace of God in vain."* (2 Corinthians 6:1)

A Burning Reformer

Josiah was faced with unprecedented evils. Through the brazen wicked heart of king Manasseh, abominations were created to defile the Temple. Now ritual booths and demonic altars were set in place. Here, perversion was engaged. Sodomy and prostitution were commonplace. Astrology was practiced. There were even ritual sacrifices of their own children offered to the false gods of Baal, Asherah, Topheth and Molech! Perversion, witchcraft and corruption were the order of the day. Josiah saw his people worshiping in temples dedicated to false pagan gods. He witnessed baby sacrifices, the unnatural perverted sex between people of the same gender and the shedding of innocent blood. These things disgusted him, and he sought The Lord in the midst of chaos and darkness.

When Josiah became 26 years of age, the Bible tells us that he met with Hilkiah, the high priest, and commissioned a housecleaning and restoration of the Temple of God.

"Now it came to pass, in the eighteenth year of King Josiah, that the king sent Shaphan the scribe, the son of Azaliah, the son of Meshullam, to the house of the LORD, saying: "Go up to Hilkiah the high priest, that he may count the money which has been brought into the house of the

LORD, which the doorkeepers have gathered from the people. And let them deliver it into the hand of those doing the work, who are the overseers in the house of the LORD; let them give it to those who are in the house of the LORD doing the work, to repair the damages of the house; to carpenters and builders and masons; and to buy timber and hewn stone to repair the house. However there need be no accounting made with them of the money delivered into their hand, because they deal faithfully."
2 Kings 22: 3-7 | NKJV

In the midst of repairs and restoration, a stunning discovery is made. Hilkiah's "find" would forever change Josiah's life and that of all of Israel! The Book of the Law is found in the Temple!

"Then Hilkiah the high priest said to Shaphan the scribe, "I have found the Book of the Law in the house of the Lord." And Hilkiah gave the book to Shaphan, and he read it. So Shaphan the scribe went to the king, bringing the king word, saying, "Your servants have gathered the money that was found in the house, and have delivered it into the hand of those who do the work, who oversee the house of the Lord." Then Shaphan the scribe showed the king, saying, "Hilkiah the priest has given me a book." And Shaphan read it before the king.

"Now it happened, when the king heard the words of the Book of the Law, that he tore his clothes. Then the king commanded Hilkiah the priest, Ahikam the son of Shaphan, Achbor the son of Michaiah, Shaphan the scribe, and Asaiah a servant of the king, saying, "Go, inquire of the Lord for me, for the people and for all Judah, concerning the words of this book that has been found; for great is the wrath of the Lord that is aroused against us, because our fathers have not obeyed the words of this book, to do according to all that is written concerning us."
2 Kings 22:8-10 | NKJV

Turned into Another Man

Can you imagine the horror and the anguish Josiah suffered at reading the Word of The Lord and realizing that the wrath of God was kindled against Israel for their disobedience and corruption? The Scriptures say that Josiah's heart was tender before The Lord, and at His Word he humbled himself and tore his clothes and wept before God!

Kings and Chronicles tell us that upon reading the Word of God, Josiah was transformed into a raging fire! With unstoppable zeal, he went down into the Temple and killed all the false priests, false teachers, false prophets, mediums and soothsayers! He tore down all the ritual booths of perversion and idols to false gods! After cleansing the Temple, he went throughout all Judea tearing down every shrine in the high places crushing and pulverizing them into powder! The Word of the Lord burned in Josiah *like a mighty fire and a hammer that crushes rocks into pieces* (Jeremiah 23:29). He executed the false priests, desecrating these sites, by burning their bones upon the altars. He cut down and destroyed the wooden idols and tore down their sacred pillars, filling them with the bones of the false priest!

Josiah didn't stop in Judah! He burned like a torch in the hand of God, cleansing all of Israel! This cleansing flame didn't stop in the southern region. It burned into the northern region of Israel where the other 10 tribes were whoring after other false gods! The entire nation underwent a reformation of the fire of His holiness, by the hand of Josiah!

2 Kings 23:3 | NKJV
"Then the king stood by a pillar and made a covenant before the Lord, to follow the Lord and to keep His commandments and His testimonies and His statutes, with all his heart and all his soul, to perform the words of this covenant that were written in this book. And all the people took a stand for the covenant."

I have a big question for you. Have you ever wondered what King Josiah read in the discovery of these lost Scriptures that made him a raging unquenchable fire? What was it that transformed him into another man so much so that he cleansed a Nation? What made him do all of that?

We've read the scriptures, right? Why are we not tearing down anything? Why are we not burning down anything? God give us Josiahs and Gideons once again! Ezekiel cries unto us afresh, for we *have set up idols in our hearts and put before us that which causes us to stumble into iniquity! (Ezekiel 14:3)*

We've lost our way! The American Church tolerates sin. We don't confront evil today, do we? And, why not? Because we don't hate sin. We tolerate it! We just play *Mr. Nice Guy.* We have far too many cowering pulpiteers who preach an anemic gospel, full of passivity, compromise and conformity. Today, we find ourselves in the midst of a famine of real leaders - voices that would preach the uncompromised Word of God. We've been seduced to mold our language into palatable messages, in order to preserve our social and political status. Our obsession today is growing crowds. Our meetings are structured to feed and inspire the masses with our favorite sugar cookies and feel-good teachings. Our hipster preachers are nothing more than entertainers today - which I affectionately call, *Dr. Feelgoods',* serving spiritual peanuts and popcorn with a side of cotton candy for the wayward flock. Many Churches cannot even discern the difference between the anointing and the adrenaline, because they've run on hype for so long. We should have learned long, long ago that hype doesn't transform lives!

I've been accused of being intense and far too passionate. I've been told that my *prophetic revival style preaching* is old fashioned and not relevant. I'm not losing sleep over those opinions. You see, I'm under an impassioned conviction that we need burning ministers of fire in the pulpits of America! I believe we need messengers with tears in their eyes and fire in their bones, calling us up out of our backslidings. We need truth that makes us free and delivers us from passivity and decay. Today, ministers cower with embarrassment to preach biblical morality, truth, integrity and self-disciple. For far too long, the church has been drowning in a narcissistic bath of self-indulgence and compromise.

John 3:19 | NKJV
"And this is the condemnation, that the light has come into the world, and men loved darkness rather than light, because their deeds were evil."

Let me go on the record and be clear! God completely and passionately loves people, but He hates sin. We need to hate what

God hates. *"You who love the Lord, hate evil! He preserves the souls of His saints; He delivers them out of the hand of the wicked."* (Psalm 97:10) Hate is a strong word! You will never cry out to God for a healing and miracle ministry, until you begin to hate and burn with hostility against sickness and disease. You will never cry out to God to raise you up to crush poverty, until you begin to hate lack and poverty. Furthermore, we'll never really deal with the sin in our own lives until we hate it. In the end, we become what our desires make us. Who we become reveals what we really desire. If you desire the praise of men, then you will become a certain kind of person. But if you desire the praises of God, then you must become fearless, in the face of the derision of scoffers and naysayers.

Cleansing Fire

I can tell you what Josiah read that made him become an unstoppable and unquenchable fire. In order to do that, we'll need to travel back in time to 1 Kings chapter 13 about 300 years before Josiah came on the scene.

At this point in history, David's son, King Solomon, is dead. Solomon's son, Rehaboam has now become the new king of Israel. Rehaboam offended the elders so they had a big "church split" and hired their own pastors. They called them *kings*. After the revolt and split, the 10 northern tribes were led by Jeroboam, who was the first king of the northern kingdom.

Jeroboam manipulated the people. He feared their return to Jerusalem for worship, as they might then return to The Lord and to Rehaboam's leadership. So he had set up a shrine, with an altar of worship to a false god, (adored with golden calves) in the city of Bethel.

1 Kings 13:1-6 | NKJV
"And behold, a man of God went from Judah to Bethel by the word of the Lord, and Jeroboam stood by the altar to burn incense. Then he cried out against the altar by the word of the Lord, and said, "O altar, altar! ***Thus says the Lord: 'Behold, a child, Josiah by name, shall be born to the house of David; and on you he shall sacrifice the priests of the high places who burn incense on you, and men's bones shall be***

burned on you.'" And he gave a sign the same day, saying, "This is the sign which the Lord has spoken: Surely the altar shall split apart, and the ashes on it shall be poured out." So it came to pass when King Jeroboam heard the saying of the man of God, who cried out against the altar in Bethel, that he stretched out his hand from the altar, saying, "Arrest him!" Then his hand, which he stretched out toward him, withered, so that he could not pull it back to himself. The altar also was split apart, and the ashes poured out from the altar, according to the sign which the man of God had given by the word of the Lord. Then the king answered and said to the man of God, "Please entreat the favor of the Lord your God, and pray for me, that my hand may be restored to me. So the man of God entreated the Lord, and the king's hand was restored to him, and became as before."

Whoa! This is stunning! Three hundred years before Josiah would be born, this prophet released Josiah's divine destiny and purpose by name! What do you think Josiah read in the scroll found in the temple of God? I believe Josiah read his very name and destiny in the pages of the book through this prophecy! If you don't believe that's true, read the rest of the story.

After Josiah had cleansed and reformed all of Israel and restored true worship to God, He made a covenant with the Lord to keep his commands, testimony and statutes, with all his heart. Amazingly, the people who were lost in darkness took a stand for the covenant and vowed to follow the Lord wholly. Josiah had now come full circle to his divine assignment and prophetic word. Look at this revelation...

2 Kings 23:15-17 | NKJV

Moreover the altar that was at Bethel, and the high place which Jeroboam the son of Nebat, who made Israel sin, had made, both that altar and the high place he broke down; and he burned the high place and crushed it to powder, and burned the wooden image. **As Josiah turned, he saw the tombs that were there on the mountain. And he sent and took the bones out of the tombs and burned them on the altar, and defiled it according to the word of the Lord which the man of God proclaimed, who proclaimed these words. Then he said, "What gravestone is this that I see?" So the men of the city told him, "It** *is the tomb of the man of God who came from Judah and proclaimed these things which you have done against the altar of Bethel."*

Prophesy fulfilled! Mission Complete! Can GOD write a story or what? Can God direct the steps of a righteous man or a righteous woman? Yes He can!

Isaiah 58:12 | NKJV
"Those from among you Shall build the old waste places; You shall raise up the foundations of many generations; And you shall be called the Repairer of the Breach, The Restorer of Streets to Dwell In."

Isaiah 61:4 | NKJV
"And they shall rebuild the old ruins, They shall raise up the former desolations, And they shall repair the ruined cities, The desolations of many generations."

Yes! Do you hear the call? Those from among us shall build, raise up, repair and restore! Reformers are those who reconstitute, level, restore and set into alignment that which had been torn apart and desolated. They burn in the passionate love of God and have pledged not to be conformed to the spirit of the age. Down through the ages, God has positioned and raised up burning passionate reformers and revolutionaries, as the times demanded, for the healing of breaches and broken places, to bring nations back into alignment with His heart. Study the lives and courage of passionate reformers such as John Wycliffe, John Hus, Martin Luther, George Fox, Scotland's John Knox and Sir William Wallace, Count Zinzendorf, John Wesley, Jonathan Edwards, George Whitfield, William Booth, John Bunyan, Charles Spurgeon, Charles Finney and William Wilberforce.

He has always worked through these consecrated vessels as they are His agents of change for human history. He sought out men and women who were willing to stand up valiantly against the forces of darkness invading our society. Deep in the reformer's spirit is the standard that they cannot accept the status quo, business as usual and things as they are. They refuse to let the world

157

around them shape and define them. They are non-conformists, and they refuse to play the games of their lukewarm generation. Reformers are not afraid to be the passionate and different ones. They have chosen to burn with holy fire! He is calling now, in these last days, for uncommon reformers of hope to join with Him in the transformation of Nations!

To those with burning hearts, I call to you by The Spirit of The Lord! God is actively raising up a company of reformers and revolutionaries to heal and restore Nations! Perhaps you too are a deliverer, whom God is calling even now, to bring freedom to the captives!

Jesus gave us our commission: *"All authority has been given to Me in heaven and on earth. Go therefore and make disciples of all the nations, baptizing them in the name of the Father and of the Son and of the Holy Spirit, teaching them to observe all things that I have commanded you; and lo, I am with you always, even to the end of the age."* Amen. (Matthew 28:18-20)

Nothing will ignite you on fire more than when your purpose is revealed! When Josiah saw his divine purpose and destiny, he became a fire that could not be quenched! Not only is Josiah's name in the book, but Jesus said your name is written in His Book of Life! Jesus told his disciples *don't rejoice that demons are subject to you but rejoiced because your name is written in the heaven.* (Luke 10:20) Our names are written in heaven! We must never forget this!

Josiah's name means, **The Fire of The Lord**! I pray that the fire of His holiness will burn in your heart with such intensity and zeal that your testimony will stand with Josiah's...

2 Kings 23:25 | NKJV
*"Now before him there was no king like him, **who turned to the Lord with all his heart, with all his soul, and with all his might,** according to all the Law of Moses; nor after him did any arise like him."*

Reformers align, reconstitute, level and balance. They repair and restore what has been broken and corrupted. Reformers bring divine order and alignment with The King's purpose and design.

A picture of divine alignment is found in the Greek word, *katartizo* - which means to adjust and put a thing back into its appropriate position. The word is used in Matthew 4:21 concerning mending nets. In 1 Corinthians Chapter 1:10 it's referred to as repairing schisms or relational breaks; and in Galatians 6:1 in restoring broken lives. The word is also used to describe the restoration of a dislocated joint or broken bone. My friend, Dutch Sheets, calls *katartizo* "God's special work as the holy Chiropractor". What I am praying and contending for is that America experiences a divine *katartizo* shift back to its God-appointed purpose and destiny!

We Need An Alignment!

Just as Josiah was used to bring a spiritual and social shift and alignment to Israel, God wants to engage each of us as atmosphere architects to set in order His dominion and overthrow every satanic system of worship. Josiah demolished the thrones of iniquity and overthrew the satanic high places of his day. He restored divine order and pure worship unto the Lord throughout his Nation. He was a reformer who brought Israel into alignment with the Word of the Lord and His covenant to His people.

The Kingdom of God was always meant to shape culture, never to retreat from it! I believe a sweeping move of God is coming like a wild fire, which will usher many into the Kingdom of God! There is an army of fire and hope-reformers, coming into alignment to restore the foundations. Many are hearing and obeying the call of the Lord to invade the darkness for spiritual and social reformation. They are the burning ones, God's agents of change. They are fearlessly pressing into the wreckage of desolation. They will restore. They will mend. They will rebuild. They understand their commission and authority. They believe that light is far greater than and superior to darkness. These firebrand carriers are the keys to societal transformation. The empowered church is not cowering in its little subculture, focusing on itself, remaining safe in its territory separated from the world. No, it is on the offensive, advancing and overcoming every adversity and obstacle, to bring the light of His glory into the darkness!

Will we seize the moment? Will those who have been in preparation be willing to risk everything to shape history? Lou Engle, a true prophet and intercessor in our times said, *"For every revolution, someone needed to preach it, praise it, print it, pray it, paint it, and promote it. In every arena of the judicial crisis for justice, God always has an Esther being prepared in the background. Where there is a Hitler, God has a Churchill. Where there's a Jezebel there is an Elijah being prepared. The only question that remains is, will the people who have been prepared seize their moments and risk everything, renouncing self-promotion to become the hinge of history."*

We are in a strategic time of alignment, even now, and reformers must valiantly surge forward in every sphere of influence throughout our Nation. May the fire of the Lord cleanse us from our sins and heal our land! Jesus is the hope of glory and the hope of the nations!

Chapter Seven

America - What Have We Become?

A merica has lost her ability to blush! Take a good look into the darkness. Don't turn your head. Keep looking until your eyes become rivers of tears. Keep looking until you are broken in the depths of your spirit. Let it break your heart. Let your wells of compassion burst. Can you see them? Can you hear them? Can you smell the stench of social decay? Our Nation is lost in a gross cloud of deception and hopelessness. Let a divine awakening of compassion shake us from our reluctance and resistance to feel the pain and agony of those lost in darkness right now!

America is under siege with scandalous corruption, homosexuality and violence. The flood of filth is everywhere we look. Our cities are filled with crime, violence, abortion, divorce, suicide, drug addiction, teen pregnancy, pornography and sexual sins. Our televisions are pouring sex and perversion into every living room. The gay and lesbian agenda is advancing in Disney programs, ABC Family, Fox affiliates and kids' channels. It is no secret that the gay community wants to indoctrinate an entire generation of American children with pro-homosexual propaganda and eliminate traditional values from American society. Their goal is to create a new America, based on sexual promiscuity, in which the values you and I cherish are long forgotten. Lesbian activist, Patricia Neal Warren, has said: "It is the first fact of civilization, whoever captures the kids owns the future." An entire generation has grown up in a society that will do almost anything for its self-indulgences. America's society is obsessed with feeling good, and conditioned to seek comfort and pleasure. This is not the future I want for America's children!

Homosexuality is no longer just in San Francisco, Seattle and New Orleans. It's not a back alley issue. It's a mainstream issue, and it's in your face. It's in our children's faces through TV, movies, video games and advertisements. Sadly, many Christian parents are asleep at the wheel so to speak - not being effective watchmen for the souls of their children. We had better wake up!

The world is changing rapidly, and truth is highly flammable and very dangerous in 2014. Moral confusion is everywhere. Truth isn't fashionable and championed in our world today. Tolerance is the banner and motto of the day. Sexual perversion and homosexuality is one of the greatest issues of our times. Anyone who stands to proclaim the truth of the Word of God, must be prepared for the venomous backlash of hate and attack.

Isn't it ironic that the media and the academic elite hold "tolerance" and "diversity" above all virtues, and yet appear unwilling to tolerate anyone who dares to claim a belief in absolute right and wrong, the absolute sanctity of human life for unborn children, the biblical definition of marriage between a man and a woman, or a God who holds men accountable for their actions? Such views are now deemed worse than politically incorrect. They have become, in fact, culturally incorrect.

A sure tipping point recently came when our President and Vice President repositioned their stance and endorsement for same sex marriage here in America. Their stance to redefine traditional biblical marriage for our society could be become devastating for our Nation's future. Ladies and gentlemen, we are in trouble! A few years ago, an American teenage girl was threatening to sue the school system, because it would not sanction her lesbian lover as her prom date. CNN interviewed this young lady and praised her courage and mourned her mistreatment. President Obama honored her at the White House, celebrating her bravery as if she was a hero.

More recently, our President was there yet again to praise and honor another pawn for the Gay & Lesbian agenda, Michael Sam, who was drafted to the NFL's St. Louis Rams. President Obama's weighed in on Michael's story saying, "...*we are taking an important step forward today in our Nation's journey.*" Sam's kiss with his gay lover, seen around the world, has now been aired on every network for all to see. Yes, I'm outraged. I'm angry!

The President's stance is wrong and immoral. He's wrong on marriage and morality in general. Period. The government didn't think up and design marriage, God did. Genesis 2:24 says, "*A man shall leave his father and mother and cleave unto his wife and the two shall become one flesh.*" The President is wrong on same sex relationships. He may be "politically correct" in this corrupt atmosphere and even "culturally relevant" for the masses, but he's wrong and it's sin. Sex is a holy union between a married man and woman. God's intent is one woman with one man for one lifetime. Sometimes things go terribly wrong in marriages. But, there is life and forgiveness after divorce. God hates divorce, but he also forgives it.

America is in the middle of a massive decision in this country as to whether we are going to embrace a path toward total secularism, which marginalizes people of faith, or whether people of faith and other persons of goodwill are going to rally to the side of those who hold to the moral and biblical values which have made this country what it is. Culture is shifting. Our country is heading down a path of moral chaos and decline. Much like Western Europe, religion is now becoming "out of fashion". Christians in this country must come to a biblical understanding of where they are with regard to the moral issues of our day—issues that relate to life and issues that relate to sexuality. Beyond the outrage, frustration and shameful disappointment in what we see in our national leaders, where are our tears? Are we broken inside? Can our heart bleed with pain for our generation, our children and those that are yet to come? Joseph Caryl, said *"According to the weight of the burden that grieves you, is the cry to God that comes from you."* Are you grieved? Our leaders are calling evil good. Our leadership is applauding abominations. We're in trouble. America has lost her way. What will it take for us to find our way back? We must have revival and awakening!

Not only have secular and political leaders lost their way, there is alarming erosion within the church spiritual leadership, which is waffling, dizzy with deception. Leaders are afraid to stand with the authority of the Word of God. This is not a republican or democratic issue. This is more than a contentious debate of discrimination. It is one of morality! This is a biblical issue that demands truth for moral clarity. Do you know what bothers me and brings a *red flag* up in my spirit? It's how strangely silent The Church is on this issue. We are afraid to discuss it, because it may be politically incorrect. The Church needs delivered from its political spirit. We are far too worried about offending anyone. The fear of man, again! We are afraid of being rejected and ostracized for standing on God's Word.

We sit quietly on mute, idly watching the cowardly ministers, who are masquerading on the television, telling America that homosexuals are going to be in heaven. The Word of God plainly and fearfully tells us, *"Do you not know that the unrighteous will not inherit the kingdom of God? Do not be deceived. Neither fornicators, nor idolaters, nor adulterers, nor homosexuals, nor sodomites, nor thieves, nor covetous, nor drunkards, nor revilers, nor extortioners will inherit the kingdom of God.* (1 Corinthians 6:9&10)

> *"In times of universal deceit, telling the truth becomes a revolutionary act."*
> George Orwell

I realize that no matter what I say here, I'm going to offend someone. I've laid aside the fantasy that everyone is going to like me or applaud the message. But if you are offended, my advice for you is that you go to Jesus and to the Word of God with your offense and see what God has to say about sexual perversion. The Word needs to be your final authority. These issues are not going away. You can ignore this cultural avalanche by putting your head in the sand, or you can choose to face it head on and overcome evil with good. The sword of the Spirit – the Word of God, spoken in love and compassion and with authority, brings change. You cannot remain silent.

Where Are Our Men & Women Of God?

Today we have so called *"leaders"* in the body of Christ who carry the *principles* of Jesus, but their personal beliefs and ministry are anything but Christ-like. It's high time that we start recognizing real leaders who are worthy to be followed, and begin denouncing the imposters who are drunk with deception and false teaching. I'm simply amazed how many teachers we have in the pulpits of America, who bear no supernatural fruit in their ministries. Many have never seen a notable healing or miracle. They've never cast out demons. They don't flow and operate in the gifts of the spirit. They're not prophetic. Sadly, many of them are not real students of the Word, and it's abundantly clear when they open their mouths. Yet, masses of people flock to these sterile churches and read their self help books. Christianity is not a behavioral modification, self-improvement or sin management program. It's the indwelling of the Spirit of God which transforms a life from the inside out. His ministry is unparalleled!

How is it that so many leaders are comfortable believing their *job* is making sermons for a living? They have put the highest premium on becoming professional communicators. They esteem teaching and expositing the principles with eloquent words, yet never bring people to a power encounter with God. They have a *"form of godliness, but deny its very power."* Their forms and formulas draw the crowds, but lack the substance. The Apostle Paul wrote, *"For the kingdom of God does not consist in talk, but in power. (1 Corinthians 4:20)* There's a lot of talking, but very little demonstration of power. Something is wrong with this. Why is it that ministries today rarely contend for the supernatural?

167

Sure, it risks ruining a reputation. Many suffer from what I call *Pneumaphobia!*

*Pnuema – Holy Spirit, Spirit of GOD, Breath of GOD *Phobia - a persistent, irrational fear of a specific object, activity, or situation that leads to a compelling desire to avoid it.

Pneumaphobia has caused many leaders to create systems to filter the atmosphere at all cost, to avoid The Spirit of God, lest they lose control of their *order*. We live in times that demand that we clarify what a true leader is in the Body of Christ. Many are being conditioned into a weak, impotent, powerless form of leadership.

Recently, I was invited by a friend to a church leadership conference. After reviewing the roster of speakers, I respectfully and simply declined. My friend asked me why I lacked interest in attending. My response somewhat surprised him. I asked him, *"What is it about these speakers that define them as leaders in your mind? Are these people really worthy to be followed? Is it because they sell large number of books in the evangelical world? Or is it the notable size of their churches?" "What about their personal beliefs and stances on moral issues?"* Let me be clear, I'm not against big churches whatsoever. I love them and our family is part of a very large congregation. However, the real crux of what I am getting at is that I had already done my research on this roster of speakers several years prior. I was continually perplexed at why people followed these types of ministries, which look nothing like the biblical stature of true ministry.

Most of these leaders were very liberal and carry a false grace message to the Church world. They openly endorsed gay marriage and voted pro-choice. One of these speakers, a very notable author, had recently performed a secret wedding in his backyard for his gay son and partner. One of the other speakers was under the persuasion of "Chrislam", a belief that Christians and Muslims serve the same God. No, we do not! Let's get real folks! Do you see the trouble we are in? We have lost our way! I don't care if a so-called "leader" has celebrity status in the body of Christ. People may even flock to buy their books and attend sterile meetings. If such leaders approve and endorse homosexuality, gay marriage and abortion - they are not leaders...they are lost. They are blind guides and imposters. Jesus warned us plainly that, *"Can a blind man guide a blind man?' Wouldn't they both end up in the ditch? An apprentice doesn't lecture the master. The point is to be careful who you follow as your teacher."* (Luke 6:39) America's pulpits and churches need more than a *touch* from God – they need His cleansing *torch*!

2 Timothy 4:3-5 | NKJV
"For the time will come when they will not endure sound doctrine, but according to their own desires, because they have itching ears, they will heap up for themselves teachers; and they will turn their ears away from the truth, and be turned aside to fables. But you be watchful in all things, endure afflictions, do the work of an evangelist, fulfill your ministry."

That time is here, ladies and gentlemen! Imposters and counterfeits are amongst us, turning aside from the truth - *deceiving and being deceived.* Man of God...woman of God...here me, follow your doctrine carefully! There is no other solid foundation than the Word of God!

Emerging leaders and revivalists, God has given us unprecedented access to more power than all the armies on the earth combined, in the Holy Spirit. Why sell yourselves short by becoming a motivational speaker? Do you want to be a polished professional or a prophetic voice? Follow the pattern that Jesus set forth to display the power of God and impart the Holy Spirit. Leaders, do not conform to the spirit of this age! Do you want to waste your life in powerless forms or step out and walk on the water of the supernatural with Jesus? We need burning leaders who are uniquely gifted to host the Presence of the Lord and equip the Church to do the supernatural works of Jesus.

America desperately needs more than hip sermonettes and empty clichéd pep talks. Jesus is the pattern for transformational ministry. If you want a supernatural ministry, let me encourage you to tap into the resurrection power of Christ and let His Word possess you that you may *be complete and thoroughly equipped for every good work.*

(2 Timothy 3:17)

God's Fire Will Cleanse

Matthew 3:3 &10-12 | NKJV

"Repent, for the kingdom of heaven is at hand!" For this is he who was spoken of by the prophet Isaiah, saying: "The voice of one crying in the wilderness: 'Prepare the way of the Lord; Make His paths straight.'"

"And even now the ax is laid to the root of the trees. Therefore every tree which does not bear good fruit is cut down and thrown into the fire. I indeed baptize you with water unto repentance, but He who is coming after me is mightier than I, whose sandals I am not worthy to carry. He will baptize you with the Holy Spirit and fire. His winnowing fan is in His hand, and He will thoroughly clean out His threshing floor, and gather His wheat into the barn; but He will burn up the chaff with unquenchable fire."

Homosexuality is an illicit lust forbidden by God. He said to His people Israel, *"You shall not lie with mankind, as with womankind: it is abomination."* (Leviticus 18:22). Abomination means: vile, shameful and detestable. The Bible also says pride, dishonest business practices, lying and causes of discord among the church is an abomination too. According to the Word of God, homosexality is a perversion. In the Bible sodomy is a synonym for homosexuality. God spoke plainly on the matter when He said, *"There shall be no whore of the daughters of Israel, nor a sodomite of the sons of Israel"* (Deuteronomy 23:17). The whore and the sodomite are in the same category. A sodomite was not an inhabitant of Sodom, or a descendant of an inhabitant of Sodom, but a man who had given himself to homosexuality, and the unnatural vice for which Sodom was known.

Romans 1:20-32 | NKJV

"For since the creation of the world His invisible attributes are clearly seen, being understood by the things that are made, even His eternal power and Godhead, so that they are without excuse, because, although they knew God, they did not glorify Him as God, nor were thankful, but became futile in their thoughts, and their foolish hearts were darkened.

170

Professing to be wise, they became fools, and changed the glory of the incorruptible God into an image made like corruptible man – and birds and four-footed animals and creeping things.

Therefore God also gave them up to uncleanness, in the lusts of their hearts, to dishonor their bodies among themselves, who exchanged the truth of God for the lie, and worshiped and served the creature rather than the Creator, who is blessed forever. Amen.

For this reason God gave them up to vile passions. For even their women exchanged the natural use for what is against nature. Likewise also the men, leaving the natural use of the woman, burned in their lust for one another, men with men committing what is shameful, and receiving in themselves the penalty of their error which was due. And even as they did not like to retain God in their knowledge, God gave them over to a debased mind, to do those things which are not fitting; being filled with all unrighteousness, sexual immorality, wickedness, covetousness, maliciousness; full of envy, murder, strife, deceit, evil-mindedness; they are whisperers, backbiters, haters of God, violent, proud, boasters, inventors of evil things, disobedient to parents, 31 undiscerning, untrustworthy, unloving, unforgiving, unmerciful; who, knowing the righteous judgment of God, that those who practice such things are deserving of death, not only do the same but also approve of those who practice them."

Homosexuality is destructive and leads to bondage. It becomes toxic and destructive to the physical body. It decays souls, leaving them callused, seared and numb. Those in its grasp are bound to a life of perversion. America's conscience has become so callused that we can hardly blush! Your body is precious to God. He created it to be the temple of the Holy Spirit. Literally, it is the abiding place of the God's glory!

"You, my brothers and sisters, were called to be free. But do not use your freedom to indulge the sinful nature..."
Galatians 5:13 | NIV

Without a doubt, there is so much at stake right now! We must stop cowering down in the dark. We must get on our face and cry out to God with unstoppable and unquenchable passion –

praying for the awakening of our Country. We must repent of our sins and wickedness, that He will be merciful and come and deliver us from the destruction and wages of sin. Oh, may America turn back to God, who alone can save, rescue and deliver our generation!

Man of God, woman of God, there can be no room for compromise in this hour! Our Nation's moral fabric is ripping at the seams! We need the fire of the Holy Spirit to light our hearts afresh! We must awaken now! We must arise and shine to fully preach the uncompromised Word of God, in which signs and wonders follow! (Romans 15:19) For the sake of millions upon millions of lost souls (children, teenagers, college students, fathers and mothers) right here in our Nation, we must not retreat from this vile darkness but arise to overcome with grace and truth! Are we brave enough to fall on our faces and beg for the Lord to lay His heart upon ours and invade our world for the sake of the lost? Oh God, light the fire again!

We now distribute condoms freely to our children in the public schools. Homosexuals parade half-naked down the streets of our nation's capital demanding special rights as a *minority*. In just 40 years, America's death culture has now slaughtered over 55 million of its unborn babies in the womb. Does this disturb you? Are you even willing to be disturbed? Who is weeping? Who can hear the cries coming up out of the cities? Where is our true leadership? Where are our fathers and mothers? Make no mistake, we cannot afford to roll over and hit our spiritual snooze button again!

According to God, the master architect, the family is the fundamental building block of society. If you have strong families, you have a strong society. I believe family is the "wineskin" or structure for sustainable and ever increasing revival. If we can restore the family, we can restore our country.

Presently, the state of the family in America continues to deteriorate. The marriage rate has fallen to an all-time low. We lead the world in divorce, and about a third of all children live in a home without a father. Our young people have been taught that getting married and having a family is not a priority. American families have never been this weak, and this is an incredibly troubling sign for the future of our nation. What will future generations of Americans be like if they do not have stable homes in which to grow up? Without a national awakening, that is a sobering thought. In 2014, nearly 41% of America babies were born out of wedlock, many to poor uneducated women who cannot support them. Are you looking into the darkness? Don't turn your face away. Let your tears flow.

Crack cocaine and meth is sweeping our Nation. Meth exploded onto the Americans drug scene in the 80's and by 2005, U.S. newspapers were calling America, *"The Meth Capitol of the World"*, sighting over 70 different American towns and cities from California to New York ablaze with the epidemic. The Midwest neighborhoods are ablaze with meth. Meth *"cooks"* are now combining the substance with chemicals such as battery acid, drain cleaner, lantern fuel and antifreeze. Intoxicating agents like marijuana are now celebrated as *freedom giving substances.* Look at the state of Colorado, which is expanding these *freedom horizons.* It's deplorable! Where are our public servants? Today, our civic leaders lust for power, prestige and financial gain at all cost - selling votes, enjoying tax payer funded vacations and lavish private jets, in the world of exploitation. There are scores of examples of America's decline, and frankly, we are in trouble! Millions of Americans live for handouts, as the spirit of entitlement has them in it's vice, all the while refusing to confront irresponsibility.

We have expelled God from our schools. We cannot even place the *Ten Commandments* on the walls of our classrooms. The God haters are at work right now within our country to make it illegal to mention the name of Jesus, carry Bibles, display religious pictures, or wear Christian emblems in schools and in the workplace. Their argument is it creates an *offensive environment of harassment.* Really?

As a nation, we are presently drowning in $17 trillion dollars of national debt, and everyday it continues to climb at a staggering trajectory, threatening an implosion of our Country as we know it. The corruption in every level of federal, state and local governments is unprecedented. Greed and power have become the seduction of our leaders. Our lack of moral and fiscal responsibility cannot be ignored any longer. The corrosive result of government handouts is now rampant in America. A population spoon-fed with entitlement and dependency, heads down the dead end path of bondage to poverty. We have become cynical, sarcastic, and scurrilous.

Blackened

America is blood thirsty for violence, decadence and witchcraft. Vampires, zombies, wizards and sorcerers are the entertainment of our day. Our Grammy Awards, which celebrate the National Academy of Recording Arts and Sciences, is supposed to recognize the outstanding achievements in American music. Yet we celebrate the most vile filth and perversion imaginable that is thrust upon our children. This year, Katy Perry displayed her openly demonic performance with "Dark Horse", in presenting herself unto Satan as an offering. Beyonce comes dancing in her g-string like a dripping whore to seduce with her illuminati husband Jay-Z. Then to top off the night, the barbaric and militant Gays and Lesbians come parading their agenda as they marched couples to center stage to be *"married"* by Queen Latifa! I don't watch the Grammy's and I don't judge those who do, but understand something; the eyes of our Nation (precious children and teenagers by the millions) are looking on, while men kiss men and women kiss women, pronounced in *"holy matrimony"*! And the crowds cheer and applaud this abomination. This kind of filth goes on year after year. The list of pawns and puppets is far too exhaustive to share.

Psalm 119:53 | AKJV
"Horror has taken hold upon me, because of the wicked that forsake Your law."

Where is the Church? Where's the outrage? Where is the sting of shame? Why aren't we weeping? Why aren't we tearing our cloths in agony and laying facedown before The Lord - calling upon Him for forgiveness - seeking His Presence to heal and revive our land? Why aren't we praying? Why are we not boldly denouncing this evil? America is not even blushing. We are cowards to remain quiet! We are cowards not to stand and openly denounce these hordes of hell! Make no mistake; this Third Great Awakening will be a very intense confrontation of evil. If you are not prepared for confrontation, and prepared to cast out demons, and have not counted the cost to fearlessly speak truth and deal with the abominations of our times, I suggest you ready yourself.

I am angry! And I'm not apologizing for it. I am utterly disgusted, and I am shaken to tears, when I think about America's youth and children. They are being enveloped by these seductive demonic hordes, invading our land. I'm baffled that our Nation openly celebrates the blasphemers and occultists. Creative artists? Please!

Some would say, *Oh Brian, get off your soap box and be quiet.* Really? Quiet? And let our children's minds be raped and perverted! No way. I refuse to be quiet! You need to get angry...*and sin not!* Why can't we see the threats that are enslaving this generation? Until we get angry about sickness and disease robbing lives, we won't contend for God. We won't be used to bring divine healing. Until we get angry about lack and poverty, we will never cry out for God to use us to break the chains and spirit of poverty! Until we get angry at sin, injustice and corruption, we can do nothing about it! Furthermore, until we become angry about the sin in our own lives, we will just tolerate it. We must *"not be overcome with evil, but overcome evil with good."* (1 Corinthians 12:21) May God give us Mordecais. When seeing the danger and destruction, may we too rip our cloths. May we don sackcloth and ashes in the midst of our cities, crying aloud and bitterly for the mercy of God! May God give us Gideons and Josiahs, who aren't afraid to tear down the false gods and altars to devils!

We feel justified and powerful to send our military into nations to stop injustices; yet we are pitifully blinded as we surrender our own Nation to the destructive injustices of filth and perversion, seducing our very own children. It's time we start confronting the evil that is flaunting itself right before us! Do you want righteous war on injustice? I'm not talking about rocket launchers and tanks. I'm talking about the weapon of truth that delivers us from destruction and makes us truly free. Let's start right here in our homeland, by warring to end on abortion and pornography! Where's our war on corruption and self-indulgence? And where is the Church?

Sadly, for the most part, it is asleep. We've become infected and polluted with sin and we too are celebrating the superstars of the world. Their anthems have become our anthems. The Church of America is lukewarm at best, thinking she has everything and is in need of nothing.

2 Timothy 4:3-5 | NKJV

"For the time will come when they will not endure sound doctrine, but according to their own desires, because they have itching ears, they will heap up for themselves teachers; and they will turn their ears away from the truth, and be turned aside to fables. But you be watchful in all things, endure afflictions, do the work of an evangelist, fulfill your ministry."

Make no mistake, imposters and counterfeits are amongst us, turning aside from the truth - *deceiving and being deceived.* They do not know the ways of God, and they are embarrassed by the moving of the Spirit. They are foolishness to them. Man of God... woman of God... hear me, follow your doctrine carefully! There is no other solid foundation than the Word of God!

Jesus' word to Ephesus and Laodicea must grip us with piercing conviction! *"You have forsaken your first love. Remember the height from which you have fallen! Repent and do the things you did at first. If you do not repent, I will come to you and remove your lamp stand from its place"* (Revelation 2:4&5). *"I know your deeds, that you are neither cold nor hot. I wish you were either one or the other! So, because you are lukewarm--neither hot nor cold--I am about to spit you out of my mouth. You say, I am rich; I have acquired wealth and do not need a thing But you do not realize that you are wretched, pitiful, poor, blind and naked. I counsel you to buy from Me gold refined in the fire, that you may be rich; and white garments, that you may be clothed, that the shame of your nakedness may not be revealed; and anoint your eyes with eye salve, that you may see. As many as I love, I rebuke and chasten. Therefore be zealous and repent. Behold, I stand at the door and knock. If anyone hears My voice and opens the door, I will come in to him and dine with him, and he with Me. To him who overcomes I will grant to sit with Me on My throne, as I also overcame and sat down with My Father on His throne."* (Revelation 3:15-21)

Isn't it sobering and painfully obvious that these messages of lukewarmness, spiritual poverty, nakedness and blindness are our present conditions of the Church here in America. This pain has caused me to fall on my face before our Holy God and cry out for mercy! To those who will zealously repent and open the door to the full flame of His love, He will come in and transform them into triumphant overcomers, and grant them unprecedented and unimaginable reward – to sit down with Him upon His Throne!

Much of the Church is spiritually dull, having fallen sleep in its community of comfort. The Church, for the most part, is no longer a power to be reckoned with. It has largely lost the respect of the masses. It is often the object of ridicule. Tragically, it has become the last place our nation would turn to for help. This must change! But God has promised, *"if My people who are called by My name will humble themselves, and pray and seek My face, and turn from their wicked ways, then I will hear from heaven, and will forgive their sin and heal their land."* (2 Chronicles 7:14) Only God can forgive and heal us! Without a doubt, our nation needs an awakening and reformation from our great God!

Psalm 119:136 | NKJV
"Rivers of water run down from my eyes, Because men do not keep Your law."

Jeremiah 4:19 | KJV
"O my soul, my soul! I am pained in my very heart! My heart makes a noise in me; I cannot hold my peace, Because you have heard, O my soul, The sound of the trumpet, The alarm of war."

Jeremiah 9:1 | NLT
"If only my head were a pool of water and my eyes a fountain of tears, I would weep day and night for all my people who have been slaughtered."

General Booth, the founder of The Salvation Army, once wrote to a group of frustrated ineffective evangelists – *"Try tears! Try tears!"* Can we weep over the condition of our Nation? Can we sit down and pause our lives and schedules like Nehemiah to weep over America's *broken down walls and burning gates*? Nehemiah mourned and he fasted. His prayers were born through weeping, mourning and fasting. His travailing prayer gave birth to a vision. And through tears and intercession, he asked what we should all be asking in this present hour - *Lord, how shall I go? Lord, give me grace and equip me with what I need to go to rebuild America!* We must mobilize, rise up and rebuild!

America's *walls* have broken down and our *gates* of authority burned. Every vile and evil abomination has flooded in and taken captive what it wishes. God searches for righteous men and women to stand before Him on the behalf of America! Just as He sought for a man in Ezekiel's day, when the sins and wickedness of Israel were raging, so He is seeking even now to avert America's judgment. In Ezekiel Chapter 22, you see that Israel was far from God... they were lewd and proud. The leaders were ravenous wolves abusing their God given power. Israel had forsaken God and the nation grew so weak, worldly and powerless that God made them a laughingstock to the secular world. He said, *"Therefore have I made thee a reproach unto the heathen, and a mocking to all countries"* (Ezekiel 22:4). The Lord grieved as He looked upon Israel's idolatry and bloodshed... corruption of institutions and pillars of government... corrupted officials... immorality... mothers and fathers forsaking their children... corruption in business and taxes... extortion and greed... defiance of God and His Word... the land was defiled because of all of these sins! Look at the priest of Ezekiel's day, they distorted the Word of God and led the nation into error. God did not want to send judgment, but desired to avert it by sending mercy upon them. So he looked for a man.

God said to Ezekiel, *"I looked for someone who might rebuild the wall of righteousness that guards the land. I searched for someone to stand in the gap in the wall so I wouldn't have to destroy the land, but I found no one.* (Ezekiel 22:30)

God said the very same thing to the prophet Jeremiah: *"Run to and fro through the streets of Jerusalem; See now and know; And seek in her open places If you can find a man, If there is anyone who executes judgment, Who seeks the truth, And I will pardon her."* (Jeremiah 5:1). He told the prophet, "I'll pardon the entire nation if I can find just one man who'll stand in the gap. All I need is a single soul who is wholly yielded to My will!"

God is still looking for men and women to build spiritual walls and stand in the gap. The United States Marine Corps is always on the lookout for *"a few good men."* The eyes of the Lord are searching and scanning the earth in order to find uncommon godly men and women who will courageously step forward and use their influence to exalt righteousness in America. That is the picture we see in Ezekiel 22. God says, *"I searched for a man among them who would build up the wall and stand in the gap before Me for the land, so that I would not destroy it"*. The "gap" is the break and the breach error, or falsehood, that has crept in, breeding satanic confusion and inviting the judgment of God. The gaps are so serious that they have imperiled and jeopardized America to the brink of destruction. Like Abraham and Moses, and ultimately like Jesus, who will stay in the place of unbroken intercession? Who will prepare the way of the Lord? God is looking for people of action. Will you weep for America? Who will cry aloud? Will you lay hold of God to awaken this nation? May you be that man! May you be that woman!

Psalms 11:3 | NIV
"When the foundations are being destroyed, what can the righteous do?"

If we've ever needed a real cleansing in the American pulpits, it's now! I know it's bold, but my burning prayer is that The Lord cleanses us from the ignorant shepherds and blind guides who are misleading the church, *like the blind leading the blind that both fall into the ditch* (Matthew 15:14).

I'm calling on those who have been with Jesus in the midst of His burning and all consuming flame! I'm calling on the reformers, rebuilders and menders! Those who are bold and courageous - anointed to raise up the foundations of many generations and repair and mend broken hearts and cities! I'm calling on the righteous remnant who have humbled themselves and have kept

179

themselves pure before the Lord to arise! I'm calling those who will take the burning flame of His love into gross darkness and bring deliverance to the captives and victory to the oppressed! I'm calling on the men and women who refuse to compromise, and have pledged themselves fully unto The Lord to demonstrate the glorious gospel! I'm calling on those who know both His Presence and His mighty power to arise and shine!

Isaiah 58:12 | NKJV
*"Those from among you Shall **build the old waste places**; You shall **raise up the foundations of many generations**; And you shall be called the **Repairer of the Breach, The Restorer of Streets to Dwell In**."*

Isaiah 61:4 | NKJV
*"And they shall **rebuild the old ruins**, They **shall raise up the former desolations**, And they shall **repair the ruined cities, The desolations of many generations**."*

We need those who are desperately hungry for God and willing to pay the price to see the spiritual transformation of our Nation. No longer can any sacrifice be too great or any reward held in higher importance than the reward of Jesus receiving His inheritance. It is absolutely critical that we awaken out of comfortable sleep! There must be a burning zeal for lost souls again!

Jesus' brutal and violent death reveals to us what the eternal worth of a lost soul truly is! Through the travailing sacrifice of His own body and blood, Jesus gave spiritual birth to sons and daughters, to all who would believe. The writer of Hebrews, whom I believe to be the Apostle Paul, reveals the pangs of birth: *"...who, **in the days of His flesh, when He had offered up prayers and supplications, with vehement cries and tears to Him who was able to save Him from death, and was heard because of His godly fear, though He was a Son, yet He learned obedience by the things which He suffered.** And having been perfected, He became the **author of eternal salvation** to all who obey Him..."* (Hebrews 5:7-9)

Did you feel that? Jesus was offering His own body - prayers, supplications, vehement cries and tears! Oh Heavenly Father,

I pray that you would break open the fountains of compassion and love deep within us for lost souls! Let a divine shaking of compassion cause our walls of reluctance and resistance, feeling the pain and agony of those lost in darkness, come tumbling down right now!

Listen to the cry of revivalist, Charles Finney ~

"A true believer will labor zealously to bring others to Jesus Christ. They will feel grieved that others do not love God, when they love him so much. And they will set themselves, often with great emotion, to persuade their neighbors to give Him their hearts. They will be filled with a tender and burning love for souls. They will have a longing desire for the salvation of the whole world. They will be in agony for individuals whom they want to have saved – their friends, relations and enemies. They will not only be urging them to give their lives to God, but they will carry them to God in the arms of faith, and with strong crying and tears beseech God to have mercy on them, and save their souls from endless burnings.

When the conduct of the wicked drives Christians to prayer and breaks them down, and makes them sorrowful and tender-hearted, so that they can weep day and night, and instead of scolding and reproaching them, they pray earnestly for them. When their actions, both oppositions and apathy drives Christians to their knees in prayer to God, with strong crying and tears, you may be certain there is going to be a revival."

The Apostle Paul writes about this place of travailing prayer, when he wrote to the Galatians. *"My little children, of whom I travail in birth again until Christ be formed in you."* (Gal 4:19)

Miles Black was the man who travailed over the soul of my Dad and my family! Have you ever wondered who was that man or woman of God who stood travailing for your soul? Whose tears cried out to God for your eternity, your destiny and purpose? While you were running wild in rebellion, whose prayers were preserving and enveloping you - bringing God's invasion to your soul?

Can we weep and travail with unbridled passion for the souls of our Nation? Can we come boldly before His throne of grace and cry out for America's awakening and reformation? The souls of

America are hanging in the balance even now. Can we weep? Can we be burdened and agonize for their release? Those who travail with God will prevail with Him! It's ok to pray with tears in your eyes and fire in your belly. He said, *"Ask of Me, and I will give You The nations for Your inheritance, And the ends of the earth for Your possession."* (Psalm 2:8) Ask Big! Do not hold back! Our ministry is reconciliation!

2 Corinthians 5:11 & 17-21 | NKJV
*"Knowing, therefore, the terror of the Lord, **we persuade men...**"*

*"Therefore, if anyone is in Christ, he is a new creation; old things have passed away; behold, all things have become new. Now all things are of God, who has reconciled us to Himself through Jesus Christ, **and has given us the ministry of reconciliation, that is, that God was in Christ reconciling the world to Himself, not imputing their trespasses to them, and has committed to us the word of reconciliation.** Now then, **we are ambassadors for Christ, as though God were pleading through us: we implore you on Christ's behalf, be reconciled to God.** For He made Him who knew no sin to be sin for us, that we might become the righteousness of God in Him.*

God's unquenchable love for humanity cries out – *Be reconciled to Me!* As Christ's ambassadors and messengers, I implore you to kneel in His burning Presence again and let Jesus light your heart aflame with passion for souls! Let him lay upon you the mantle of intercession. May your heart be quickened in the night hours to arise and pray! May the tears of liquid love pour down your cheeks again! Do not lose hope. Position yourself with The Intercessor – Christ Jesus our Lord who *"divided the spoil with the strong. Because He poured out His soul unto death, And was numbered with the transgressors, and bore the sins of many. And made intercession for the transgressors."* (Isaiah 53:12) I pray that you whoever you are reading this book that you will be consumed with God's holy and uncontainable passions for lost souls!

Can we pray that the fire of God will fall upon our lives afresh? Can we pray that the burning torch of God's heart and holiness will light our churches again? Can we tarry at all cost for our Nation's ultimate comeback? Can we be consumed and consecrated for Him alone? We must! Someone must weep! Someone must cry out! Someone must become an agent of transformation and awakening! I pray it will be YOU!

The Gift of Tears & Prevailing Prayer

"They weep as they go to plant their seed, but they sing as they return with the harvest."
Psalm 126:6 | NLT

We are heading into even greater difficulty and perilous times here in America. The judgments that we are presently seeing are man's selfish revolt and mutiny against divine order. We are suffering unprecedented consequences for rejecting our Loving Heavenly Father - defiling ourselves by rejecting His Son! All of creation is groaning for the end of evil and for a new day to dawn, with The King of this planet ruling in righteousness and justice. (Romans 8)

One of the greatest gifts that The Lord has renewed in me is the *gift of tears*. More recently, after two decades of ministry, Bren and I have just transitioned from Pastoring in Florida. Having placed new lead pastors in the Church, which we pioneered 10 years ago, we relocated our family and ministry to Ohio, now positioning ourselves for this coming awakening and reformation. In this time of transition, my prayer time has been kindled by tears of spiritual hunger, brokenness and grief over the world's upheaval and chaos. Specifically, my heart has been burning as Holy Spirit has restored the gift of tears to intercede for our Nation's ultimate comeback.

It's no secret that there are so many, many, many tragedies that we see daily taking place in our communities. Our national news outlets give witness to such bleak stories. Frankly, man without God is ugly! These tragedies are real sources of anger and frustration. That being said, I believe in a real sense that we need to be angry at our present social conditions and injustices. However, our anger must drive us to our knees to pray earnestly and proclaim for *His kingdom to come and His will to be done.*

We must be patiently committed for the long haul, for the process of repairing and restoring the land. For me personally, the restoration of brokenness over our country and having the ability to weep for the unborn, for the inner cities, for our famine of leadership, for our rebellion, corruption and idolatries is paramount! I believe real travailing prayer is the place where The Lord lays His heart upon ours, and we see and experience His pain and emotions; we experience the agonizing depths of mankind's betrayal of our gracious and loving Father.

God's will towards us is GOOD! Remember the angel's announcement to the shepherds heralding the arrival of the Son of God in Bethlehem, *"Glory to God in the highest, and on earth peace, good will toward men."* (Luke 2:14) From the very beginning, this was God's intention, heralded for all generations – *"peace and goodness to mankind".*

Through the cleansing power of many tears, I can see more clearly. We have abandoned our First Love and have hindered and harmed generations to come. We have shrouded the gift of His peace and goodwill towards us. In our own rebellion and profound rejection of His good pleasure, we have broken the heart of God again and again. America's only hope is to return to JESUS – *the hope of the nations!* (Matthew 12:21)

My prayer is that in the moments taken to read this book, you will find it possible to break from the busyness of life – pausing to crawl up into the eyes of our Savior, and weep for America. May you see what He sees. May you feel what He feels. May you dream His dream and give yourself fully to His vision and desires. Furthermore, I pray that this time will propel you into a place of prayer, where the depths of Father's love can break open your depths to weep for the prodigal Nation again! May the Holy Spirit open your ears to hear the cries coming up out of our cities. Lost souls are crying out in agony to be saved from their darkness. God is not calling us to a new season of prayer. He's calling us to a lifestyle of prayer to bring deliverance to the captives!

An Army of Burning Ones

In the early 1900's, reformer and evangelist, General William Booth, the founder of The Salvation Army, shared a vision he had received from the Lord, as He showed him the desperate condition of those who were lost without God. Within this vision, The Lord revealed to him the indifference and utter lack of interest that most Christians have for lost souls. In his message, "Who Cares?", William thunders passionately this appeal to believers:

> "You must do it! You cannot hold back. You have enjoyed yourself in religion long enough. You have had pleasant feelings, pleasant songs, pleasant meetings and pleasant prospects. There has been much of human happiness, much clapping of the hands and shouting of praises, very much of heaven on earth.
>
> Now then, go to God and tell Him you are prepared as much as necessary to turn your back on it all, and that you are willing to spend the rest of your days struggling in the midst of these perishing multitudes, whatever it may cost you! You must do it! With the light that is now broken in your mind, and the call that is now sounding in your ears, and the beckoning hands that are now before your eyes, you have no alternative. To go down among the perishing crowds is your duty. Your happiness from now on will consist in sharing their misery, your ease in sharing their pain, your crown in helping them to bear their cross, and your heaven in going into the very jaws of hell to rescue them! Now, tell me, what will you do?"

Yes, the question thunders loud and clear...**what will we do?** We must be intentional and deliberately willing to go into the darkness, at any cost, and carry the perishing to His loving and saving arms. We must partner with The Holy Spirit to rescue and bring deliverance to the captives and healing to the broken! We must fearlessly herald His kingdom as messengers of life and truth! We must stop at nothing to save the lost with the grace and love of Jesus Christ! We must answer the call to enter into His work of the harvest of mankind!

Jesus said, *"The harvest truly is plentiful, but the laborers are few. Therefore pray the Lord of the harvest to send out laborers into His harvest."* (Matthew 9:37&38)

CHAPTER EIGHT

WHERE ARE WE GOING?

(Revival, Awakening & Reformation)

*Father God, I pray, according to your everlasting mercies,
faithfulness and loving kindness; revive us and give America a
Third Great Awakening! A sweeping and transforming move of
Your Spirit from coast to coast…from the Carolinas to
California…from the Beaches of Florida
to the mountains of Alaska!*

Revival and awakening occurs when God's saturating presence takes hold of society and there is a tangible awareness of His nearness everywhere! I believe a Third Great Awakening (a divine invasion from heaven) is coming to our Nation which will surpass anything we have ever conceptually imagined God capable of accomplishing in our times! God is going to lay hold of Hollywood, Vegas, Wall Street, DC, Seattle, New Orleans, Detroit & Philly… God's burning love will melt the hardness of hearts like wax before the flame! We cannot underestimate His desire to consume us in His jealous fiery love!

Throughout our history, America has been marked and shaped by awakening and the outpouring of the Holy Spirit. Revival has been the hallmark of influence that ignited godly change in our society. Our history cries out to us to remember our rich heritage and the powerful sweeping moves of God of the 18th and 19th centuries.

The roots of revival that gave birth to The First Great Awakening in Great Britain and the colonies of America can be traced in the holy firestorm of Germany. Count Nikolaus Ludwig Von Zinzendorf founded a community called Herrnhut (The Lord's Watch) in 1724 in the province of Moravia. This was a pure movement of prayer and devotion. Zinzendorf and his disciples began a prayer meeting that lasted 100 years, 24 hours a day! Together, this community of believers committed to designated prayer and intercession time slots throughout each day, praying that the gospel might reach the unconverted throughout the entire earth. The Moravians sent out two types of missionaries; those to win the lost, and those to win the Church.

Great Britain's Anglican cleric, John Wesley, was deeply impacted through the Moravians. On January 1st, 1739, John Wesley gathered friends to pray through the night. Little did he know, that night of intercession would become the epicenter of ground shaking impartation to change the course of British and American history. Wesley famously recorded in his Journal: *"About three in the morning as we were continuing instant in prayer the power of God came mightily upon us in so much that many cried out for exceeding joy and many fell to the ground"*. This encounter impacted John's life profoundly and became the catalyst that ignited his heart for deeper intercession. John's friend, George Whitfield, was also a firebrand. Together, John Wesley, George Whitfield and John's brother, Charles, were the catalysts that would continue to impact Europe and North America for generations to come - even to this day. Each of them in their own right became extraordinarily used by God – John in teaching, George in preaching and Charles' gift for composing some of the greatest hymns of all time.

In 1741, Enfield, New England, was torched by the fire of God in a remarkable revival led by Jonathan Edwards. Jonathan was not only a brilliant theologian and philosopher, he was a carrier of the fire of God and a pioneering heart. On Sunday, July 8th, Edwards preached the historical message, *"Sinners In The Hand Of An Angry God"* and the fear of the Lord gripped the people. The congregation began to see themselves desperately and hopelessly lost, dangling over the leaping fires of hell. Jonathan's message was intense. Soon the people were screaming, crying out and some even fainting. Edwards had to try and regain order in the Sanctuary and quiet them, just so his message could be heard. People were clinging to the pews, while others took hold of the pillars in the church, so they wouldn't slip into hell.

Though his preaching was not dynamically charismatic, His word and ministry were fueled with the burnings of God's righteousness and holiness, so that his hearers understood that they were lost without the grace of God.

The First Great Awakening here in America was ignited by these three hallmarks: having a personal relationship with God, living with conviction and pursuing personal holiness. From 1730-1745, fifty thousand people encountered Christ in salvation. At that time there were only around two million people in the American colonies. In the mid 1730's New England began to experience atmospheric change, largely due to the preaching of Wesley. When revivalist, George Whitfield arrived from England, his ministry advanced the awakening like pouring gasoline on a fire!

During the first half of the 1800's, the population of the United States grew from five to thirty million, and the boundary of the nation moved ever westward. Revivals became the primary means of perpetuating the gospel in the growing and expanding population. These revivals at the beginning of the nineteenth century became known as the Second Great Awakening.

Cane Ridge, Kentucky became a hot spot of the Second Great Awakening, as God's Presence shook the frontier in 1801. More than twenty five thousand people gathered (more than 10% of Kentucky's population at that time) in the frontier for unending days of encountering the Presence of the Lord. Multiple preachers would find wagons, stumps or fallen trees for their pulpits to preach to the masses at the same time. Listen to the eye-witness report of this man; *"The noise was like the roar of Niagara. The vast sea of human beings were agitated as if by a storm. I counted seven ministers all preaching at once from stumps, fallen trees and wagons. Some were singing, some were praying; some piteously crying for mercy, and others shouting most vociferously. I became as weak as a kitten and fled to the woods. After some time I returned to the scene of excitement, the waves of which, if possible, had risen still higher. The same awfulness of feeling came over me. I stepped up on a log where I could have a better view of the surging sea of humanity. The scene that then presented itself to my mind was indescribable. At once I saw at least five hundred swept down in a moment as if a battery of a thousand guns had been opened upon them and then immediately followed by shrieks and shouts that rent the very heavens. My hair rose upon my head. My whole frame trembled; the blood ran cold in my veins and I fled for the woods a second time..."*

"On Sabbath (Sunday) night I saw about one hundred candles burning at once – and I suppose, one hundred persons of all ages from eight to sixty years at once on the ground crying for mercy...The sensible, the weak, learned and unlearned, the rich and the poor are the subjects of it."

"Sinners dropping down on every hand, shrieking, groaning, crying for mercy, convoluted," one witness said, *"professors [believers] praying, agonizing, fainting, falling down in distress for sinners, or in raptures of joy! Some singing, some shouting, clapping their hands, hugging and even kissing, laughing; others talking to the distressed, to one another, or to opposers of the work, and all this at once."*

Exhilarating isn't it! The Spirit of God came in power sweeping them to the ground and baptizing many with the Holy Spirit and with fire. Transformation came to that entire region of America as Love came down!

The Cane Ridge Outpouring quickly became one of the best-reported events in American history, and according to Vanderbilt historian Paul Conkin, "arguably ... the most important religious gathering in all of American history." It ignited the explosion of evangelical religion, which soon reached into nearly every corner of American life. For decades the prayer of camp meetings and revivals across the land was "Lord, make it like Cane Ridge."

192

What is notable, is the outpouring at Cane Ridge carried the same distinctions and qualities of the Great Awakening of the 1740s, and of the revivals in medieval Europe, and of the day of Pentecost in first century Jerusalem. All were moments when heaven invaded and people fell, whirled, praised and groaned - being overwhelmed in a wild, messy, and unimaginable way. These were times of profound encounter.

Awakening in The Marketplace

New York City was ignited in 1857 as a great prayer revival emerged. God raised up a quiet, zealous, retired businessman named, Jeremiah Lanphier. Jeremiah was consumed with the eternal burnings of God's heart for His city and in an act of obedience to the Spirit's wooing he began to promote a weekly, *"Lunch Hour Prayer Meeting"* for revival. Six people attended the first meeting; twenty-five for the second. But within just several months, tens of thousands were praying several days a week around the clock! This prayer revival spread rapidly from city to city. Some mark this prayer revival from New York as the flame that leapt across the ocean to England, Ireland and then Wales, where it literally shaped the destiny of that nation.

This fire for prayer was spreading to Chicago as 2,000 men met at noon for prayer gatherings in Metropolitan Hall. Philadelphia's Jayne's Hall was packed with 4,000 men who were meeting for prayer. Indeed, a thousand met daily in Louisville, Kentucky. By March 1858, newspapers carried front-page reports of over 6,000 attending daily prayer meetings in New York, 6,000 attending them in Pittsburgh. Daily prayer meetings were held in Washington, at five different times, to accommodate the crowds.

From 1857 to 1858 America experienced a wave of mass salvations! Over 1 Million (non-church members) were born again, in addition to the 1 Million who were saved in churches, that had been playing religious games. At the height of this revival there were over 50,000 people coming into the kingdom a week! This revival that swept into Chicago was the catalyst that gave birth to D.L. Moody's 40 year ministry! Within a decade, slavery was legally abolished!

Mary Stuart Relfe, in her book, The Cure Of All Ills, said: "The revival of 1857 restored integrity to government and business in America once again. There was renewed obedience to the social commandments. An intense sympathy was created for the poor and needy. A compassionate society was re-birthed. The reins of America were returned to the godly. Yet another time, Revival became the solution to the problems, the remedy for the evils, the cure of all ills."

Edwin Orr, in his book, The Light Of The Nations, said: "Undoubtedly the greatest revival in New York's colorful history was sweeping the city, and it was of such an order to make the whole nation curious. There was no fanaticism, no hysteria, simply an incredible movement of the people to pray."

Pioneers

During the Second Great Awakening, God ignited the 29 year old lawyer named Charles Finney. Finney became one the leading firebrand revivalists of the 19th century. His voice was an anointed fire, hammer and sword! *"When he opened his mouth he was aiming a gun. When he spoke, bombardment began. The effects of his speaking were almost unparalleled in modern history. Over half a million people were converted through his ministry ... in an age when there were no amplifiers or mass communications, he spearheaded a revival which literally altered the course of history."* Finney's ministry was undoubtedly the catalyst that ignited the 1857 Revival. He was a burning unquenchable torch, which would not bow down to the cowardly clergy of the day, who were offended by his intensity. As clergy denounced his energetic and direct preaching, Finney's evangelistic fervor grew with resolve and power. Finney and Daniel Nash (who was a mighty intercessor and friend to Finney) shook cities and regions with the Word of God, where thousands were saved - signs and wonders following.

Studying this pioneer, it becomes clear that Finney was a man of deep prayer. His ministry was marked with early morning intercession, long before the sun would come up. He often prayed from 4am to 8am. Finney would often fast all day before his night services.

Peter Cartwright was one of Finney's burning contemporaries and a circuit rider during the Second Great Awakening. Cartwright was originally from Kentucky, but moved to Illinois and was used by God to win thousands to Christ. His nickname was "God's Plowman". His unique journey led him to election to the lower house of the Illinois General Assembly in 1828 and 1832. In 1846, Abraham Lincoln notably defeated Cartwright for a seat in the United States Congress. Cartwright was known for his powerful charismatic ministry and he personally baptized more than twelve thousand new converts as a circuit rider. Finney and Cartwright's passionate soul winning ignited fires, which produced revivalists everywhere they went.

When Alexis de Tocqueville, the French political thinker and historian and author of *Democracy In America*, traveled throughout Western societies to analyze living standards and social conditions, as well as their relationship to the market and state, Alexis said this concerning America in the 1800's:

"I sought for the greatness and genius of America in her commodious harbors and her ample rivers – and it was not there . . . in her fertile fields and boundless forests and it was not there . . . in her rich mines and her vast world commerce – and it was not there . . . in her democratic Congress and her matchless Constitution – and it was not there. **Not until I went into the churches of America and heard her pulpits aflame with righteousness did I understand the secret of her genius and power. America is great because she is good, and if America ever ceases to be good, she will cease to be great."**

Oh, how we need the fire of God in our pulpits again! Oh how we need pioneers and burning revivalists! It would be humiliating to see what Alexis de Tocqueville would write of today's modern pulpits. We have produced tame and polished communicators who have all the right moves. Professional leaders and administrators...highly organized, inspirational and motivational...but many lack the genuine touch of God. Where is the encounter of the Spirit, which should light them aflame? Where are the courageous burning men and women of God? It's worth saying again; have you ever noticed that Jesus' ministry never gave birth to great motiva-

195

tional speakers? His ministry was radical, raw and alive! Jesus' ministry gave birth to revolutionaries, world changers and reformers! They cast out devils and healed the sick. They turned cities upside down. They confronted evil at all cost!

Something is terribly amiss with ministries today. Many of our cool hipster ministers in the pulpit have never cast out a demon, never seen a healing or notable miracle in their ministries. Many of today's leaders are inspirational communicators not burning messengers and ambassadors of the kingdom. Others are merely the custodians and overseers of church campuses and properties, rather than stewards of burning houses of continual prayer, worship and equipping the saints for ministry. They are cowards in the pulpit, shallow in the Word and absolutely unwilling to confront the evils of our day. They avoid anything that's deemed "controversial" at all cost. They desire a respectable ministry that will draw the crowds. Crowds are today's motivations. Oh how we need true voices and shepherds!

It's hard to believe in 2014 how many churches are satisfied with so little of God's Presence in their midst. The church has become quite content in our one-hour services, with entertainment, cutting edge light presentations, fog machines and coffee shops. We're high on adrenaline, but low on anointing. The flame is barely flickering in many Churches, and if you bring it to their attention be ready for the backlash. Religious people protect their territory and insulate themselves well from being challenged. Those content with their forms and structures, without power, avoid any message that disturbs their sleep! Let me encourage you, as you see those who continue to reject the wooing of the Spirit, leave them quickly and press forward to feed and nourish the hungry hearts. Go, fan them into full flame. Love those who merely tolerate you, but don't waste your energy in the sterile atmosphere of religious games.

Holy Fire

At the beginning of the 20th century, Los Angeles, California became the match head of the fire of God in a humble place called Azusa Street. Scores of amazing books have been written about the outpouring of the Spirit which transformed millions of lives here in

2

our nation and the world! Pentecost fire ignited with the baptism and gifts of the Holy Spirit. It reached far and wide, throughout California, Kansas, Wales, Eastern Europe, India, and Korea.

The Azusa Street Revival of 1906, led by William Seymour, was an outpouring of epic proportions! As America was coming out of it's pioneer days and entering the industrial age, the Holy Spirit was poured out afresh upon the Church, in a new dawning of power! The baptism of the Holy Spirit and fire was deluged upon hungry and thirsty souls. Azusa became a rallying point of prayer and encounter, where people from all over the earth came to experience the manifest Presence. The fire of the Lord was imparted to the four corners of the planet by those who carried the burning coals of Azusa! Today, more than 600 million Pentecostals and Charismatic believers trace their roots to the dirt floor of 312 Azusa Street's horse stable, where the fire of God's love was poured out in encounters, miracles, healings and wonders!

One particular story from the Azusa Revival that always *wrecks* me is of a young Mexican-American man named David Garcia. David was 18 years old at the time of the Outpouring at Azusa. He lived in downtown Los Angeles, about a half mile from Grand Central Station. Garcia walked past the train station everyday on his way to the Azusa Street Warehouse. One evening, he ran into the meeting to find Frank Bartleman and told him that he needed to get to Grand Central Station immediately! While trying to catch his breath, he told Frank, "You must come now to see this"! Together they made their way to the Station as quickly as they could. This was the scene: through the entire day, people had been exiting the trains, coming from all over the world. As they tried to walk across the platform, all they could do was to fall out everywhere, under the weightiness of God's Presence. They were filled with the Holy Spirit and speaking in tongues. Garcia described, *"It looked like a disaster zone."* For several city blocks around the Azusa warehouse, people were being healed, falling out in the Spirit and receiving the baptism of The Spirit. But according to Frank Bartlemen, this was the first time The Presence had spread this far from the warehouse with such notable manifestation. Wouldn't you like to see this captured on CNN or FoxNews this afternoon? Newsflash: Los Angeles encounters overpowering force downtown, as people can no longer walk and are speaking in unknown languages!

This reminds me of a summer day in 1994, in downtown Louisville, Kentucky. I witnessed a remarkable site much like this account from Azusa, as the glory of God was pouring down so forcefully that it shut down city blocks, as thousand poured out of the International Civic Center, inebriated and overcome with joy in the Presence of God! Hundreds of people were lying in the park grass, over parked cars and hanging onto light polls to steady themselves. The downtown police on horseback had to stop and redirect traffic flow for more than an hour, because the masses could barely function under His Presence! It was stunning...Like Peter on the day of Pentecost, many were telling the police, *these are not drunk as you suppose but this is that spoken by the prophet Joel, 'And it shall come to pass in the last days, says God, That I will pour out of My Spirit on all flesh; Your sons and your daughters shall prophesy, Your young men shall see visions, Your old men shall dream dreams. And on My menservants and on My maidservants I will pour out My Spirit in those days; And they shall prophesy.* (Camp Meeting, July 1994, Louisville KY with Rodney Howard-Browne)

Does that make your heart burn, friend? God wants to invade and awaken our inner cities with His glory!

The Jesus and Charismatic movements during the 1960's and 70's, were times of great outpouring, as millions came to Christ. Throughout the Jesus movement, which ignited on the west coast in California, hippies (affectionately called Jesus Freaks & Jesus People) were coming to Christ everywhere, primarily on college campuses and in the streets. The 60's witnessed the assassinations of JFK, Martin Luther King Jr. and Bobby Kennedy, which led to the collapse of our Nation's hope and the surrender of its innocence. It was a time of inflamed rebellion, anger and violence. In the midst of upheaval and chaos, racial turmoil and the Vietnam War, drugs and "free love", exploding in mainstream culture, God was sweeping through pouring out His Spirit across our land, igniting and capturing a generation with His fire! Many of these "Jesus Freaks" went on to pioneer dynamic churches, ministries, bible schools and coffee houses. This movement stretched from coast to coast, expanding worship, igniting power evangelism and heralding the signs and wonders movements!

In the 90's, millions of people were impacted in a fresh wave of renewal and revivals with Rodney Howard-Browne in Lakeland, Florida, The Toronto Outpouring, The Brownsville Revival in Pensacola, Florida and Morning Star in Charlotte, NC. Each served as a catalyst of joy, fresh fire, harvest and power that impacted far beyond even the Pentecostal and Charismatic circles. More recently, Bethel Church in Redding California and the International House of Prayer (known as "IHOP") in Kansas City, have become the flagships of sustained and increasing outpouring and launching pads for emerging revivalists! (I am deeply thankful for the personal impact that each of these ministries have had in my life and in that of my wife!)

Where Do We Stand?

While we give honor and thanks to God for our heritage and the mighty outpouring of the Spirit from days gone by, revival and awakening is simply not enough. Stay with me here. I believe we are going to see multiplied millions brought into the kingdom in just the next few years, here in America. I believe the harvest is ripe! However, we must have a vision that surpasses revival and awakening, which shifts us into cultural reformation.

Right now, we must pay close attention and take heed of where we stand as a Nation, because we are surely at a crossroads! As a Nation, we have turned away from God. We have lost our identity, because we have forsaken the true fear of The Lord. America has arrogantly mocked The Word and the ways of God. The consequence will be terrifying. This generation is presently living under a thick demonic cloud of spiritual blindness and apathetic stupor. We'd better sober up and recognize that without God, we are sunk! If we don't take a good look at where we really are, and face reality America, we won't see reformation! We cannot forget the Lord our God!

> *"The wicked shall be turned into hell, And all the*
> *nations that forget God.*
> **Psalm 9:17 | NKJV**

> *"For the nation and kingdom which will not serve you*
> *shall perish, And those nations shall be utterly ruined."*
> **Isaiah 60:12 | NKJV**

We must remember that God is faithful to His own Word! America has come to the point of believing that she can dishonor and reject God and His ways, yet still ask for His blessings. What a gross deception! God clearly said, the *nations that reject Him, will come to ruin*. If we do not aim for reformation, we are headed for sure ruin.

In Jeremiah Chapter 2, God rebuked Israel for straying far from Him. He told Jeremiah to go into the midst of Jerusalem and weep aloud, reminding them of the beauty of their youth, when they walked before the Lord in holiness. He rebuked them for worshipping worthless idols. He reminded them that He was the One who brought them out of bondage into a prosperous and bountiful land, yet they traded the true glory of God in exchange for those false gods. Indeed, not even gods at all. He told them the heavens were standing in awe and in shock, as their backsliding and apostasy had become a horror! God said that His people had abandoned Him, and He was their only true fountain of living water...yet they had dug for themselves broken and cracked cisterns that hold no water at all. (Jeremiah 2:1-13) I shudder when I read this lament, because I see America! God's heart is broken and grieved as we have forsaken Him. We have become grossly arrogant, stiff necked and obstinate and have rejected the ways of the Lord. America cannot go on courting God's favor and provision, yet refusing His lordship. I believe our prayer at this moment in time cannot simply be, "God Bless America". Rather, it *must* be, "Jesus Save America!"

What Happened?

We have just come through the greatest century of revival the world has ever seen. From the days of the Azusa Outpouring, with each following wave of Pentecostal and Charismatic movement, with the gifts of the Spirit and signs and wonders... there has been an amazing and astounding release of the kingdom. However, it's clearly not enough! In the last century the earth has been covered with blood, stemming from two World Wars, the Holocaust, the Korean War, Communism, the Vietnam War, the killing fields of South East Asia, the genocide of the Balkans and Rwanda, Islamic extremism and 55 million unborn babies sacrificed in America alone. Something is wrong here!

In spite of the Charismatic Movement and The Jesus People Movement of the 60's and 70's, a sexual revolution has exploded. A vile flood of promiscuity and pornography has been unleashed upon America. Drug abuse has exploded and sexually transmitted diseases have ravaged our society. How is it, from the time of the Welsh and Azusa Outpourings, America has experienced the greatest century of renewal and revival, yet we presently see far greater sin, corruption and debauchery across our nation? Something is wrong with this picture! What in the world happened?

In the last century, revival was awesome, yet our Nation has grown darker! Revival wasn't enough. Tragically, we didn't see the bigger picture. Perhaps God has more in mind than renewal and revivals. God is after discipling the nations! Those that know me, personally, know that I love revival! I am passionate for souls, awakening, signs and wonders. But, we desperately need the Lord to open our eyes to see something far beyond revival! We cannot move forward with a mindset that only seeks the next "Brownsville" or the next "Toronto Outpouring". Our goal should not be how many people we can pack into our churches, but rather how many we can empower and release into the Father's heart to go change the world! (No I'm not against big churches, so don't miss the point!) Societal transformation can only occur when the Church moves out of its Sunday insulated habitats and enters into all sectors of cul-

201

ture, to disciple the nations. May God lift our vision higher!

Capturing The Mountains

In 1975, Loren Cunningham, the founder of Youth With A Mission (YWAM), a global missionary organization, was in prayer, seeking the Lord for a strategy to transform the world. Loren saw 7 "mind molders" that the Holy Spirit highlighted to him.

1. Church
2. Family
3. Education
4. Government & Law
5. Media (tv, radio, internet)
6. Arts (entertainment & sports)
7. Business.

He saw that there must be a strategic invasion of Christians, rising to key positions in these territories of influence, in order to plant Immanuel's flag!

The day after he received this revelation, Loren had a meeting with Dr. Bill Bright, leader of Campus Crusade for Christ. To Loren's surprise, Bill shared that he had received a special word on concentrated areas. He called them, "world kingdoms", designed to win the nations back to God. Their word was one and the same!

More recently, in the last several years, Lance Wallnau and many other messengers have articulated the release of the 7 Mountains mandate, with amazing wisdom and revelation. The 7 Mountain revelation helps to strategically identify the sphere in which God has anointed and appointed each of us to shift culture. These mountains of influence are precisely where the enemy is attempting to shape the worldview of the masses. Look at the battleground of the media, the educational system, the political and financial systems. They are enormous – influential! The Apostle Paul explained this truth in 2 Corinthians 4:4, *"...whose minds the god of this age has blinded, who do not believe, lest the light of the gospel of the glory of Christ, who is the image of God should shine on them."* The *prince of the air* has been allowed to broadcast his territorial deception for far too long!

God's desire is to transform the global culture through His agents of change, revealed in those who can be trusted on mountain peaks of influence. The invasion of the kingdom of God, to establish His dominion in the high places, must become our divine obsession, if we can ever expect to see cultural reformation.

Invasion - Everyone Must Do Their Part!

Matthew 28:19 | NKJV
Jesus said, *"Go therefore and make disciples of all the nations, baptizing them in the name of the Father and of the Son and of the Holy Spirit, teaching them to observe all things that I have commanded you; and lo, I am with you always, even to the end of the age."*

Notice that Jesus commanded us not just to make converts in the nations. He commanded us to disciple nations! Nothing has set my hope aflame more than ingesting this revelation and divine strategy on taking the 7 Mountains. Hearts are blooming everywhere with intention to fulfill their God given calling, whether it's teaching in an elementary school, serving as a fire fighter in their community, coaching a college football team, opening businesses as an entrepreneur, dancing in the arts, or serving in government. Ministry isn't simply for those who aspire to Christian leadership within the church. In fact, focusing all ministry on the religion mountain, hinders us from seeing the bigger picture of invasion. Every believer is in full-time ministry! You are not compromising your high call because you are "outside" the church, occupying your sphere. You do not need a pulpit in a sanctuary to validate your ministry. Some are called to the church mountain, but the majority are not. Though I have served the church mountain for more than 20 years, as a pastor and a revivalist, my calling is by no means superior to anyone. What's important is that we identify where we are specifically anointed to serve and transform. You're anointed to go change the world, bringing the dominion of the Lord Jesus Christ, by serving and demonstrating His power!

There are seven key areas in which the enemy seeks to establish mind control. His goal and aim is to disciple the nations! Satan also heard the Lord's command of Matthew 28:19, and he's been active and off to the races, while the church has been satisfied to keep having revival meetings. The enemy does not mind us rallying to the church and running from revival meeting to revival meeting. Please understand, I love revival! The challenge we face in our present mode of operation is that God's purpose - pouring out His Spirit and creating encounters - has never been to "park" us in a revival culture, but to launch us into the high places of influence, so that we might change the world! If we capture the high places, we can shape culture! People have parked far too long. Believe me, I'm into burning and soaking and praying in hotspots with other believers! The last 20 years of my life have been immersed in revival culture everywhere. God has wonderfully used us (my wife and I), as catalysts in that sphere. However, I'm looking at the spiritual landscape of America, and I'm soberly aware that we need burning believers, taking His presence into the high places far beyond the borders of church culture.

For far too long, the church has been satisfied with taking the gospel only to the poor (which is absolutely critical – Matthew 25:35-39), yet it has completely forgotten about taking its power to the rulers and world authorities. We need a company of believers, which is prepared and ready to invade Washington. We need more than intercessors; we need righteous and uncompromising Christians to run for the senate, the bench, and state government. Can you picture firebrand Christians invading Hollywood, Wall Street, Entertainment and Fashion? Can you see them transforming the Rock n Roll and hip-hop community? Can you see musicians writing anointed anthems about justice and rescuing children? Can you see a generation of young people taking their talents and shaking our nation as a voice for transformation? Can we believe for abortion to be abolished in our lifetime? Can we believe for human trafficking to be annihilated? I see an invasion of courageous pioneers beginning to take elected offices, occupying the influential seats of power, stages in business, media and sports! God is looking for Esthers, Daniels, Nehemiahs and Josephs, who can operate in the gifts of the Spirit right in the enemy's house and territory. The majority of the spiritual gifts (words of knowledge, discernment of spirits, words of wisdom, prophesy) are given for the invasion of territory - the places where the church must now go!

Answer the call and your God given assignment! A call to write music and glorify God in the arts is just as important as a call to be an evangelist. Your call to home school your children and raise godly sons and daughters is just as important and honorable as answering the call to serve Zimbabwe as a missionary. Do your part to advance the kingdom with integrity, excellence and creativity!

God may call you into a place that looks ridiculous to the natural eye, but remember, sometimes the door to the miraculous looks ridiculous on the outside. Don't be afraid to walk through the door. People may criticize you and fail to understand, or perceive the lane God has called you to for this hour. My advice, forgive them quickly and keep walking.

Proverbs 22:29 | NKJV
"Do you see a man who excels in his work? He will stand before kings; He will not stand before unknown men."

The Lord said, *"I will build my church and the gates of hell will not prevail against it."* (Matthew 16:18) He has given us the keys to the kingdom. We can and we must change our way of thinking. Like Caleb of old, who had a different spirit, we too must take Immanuel's flag to seize our mountain! Ask the Lord, *"What is my mountain?" "Where have you anointed and appointed my purpose?"* It may be more than one. Don't be afraid if it is. Take time to prayerfully consider how God wants to strategically use you in discipling America or your nation. What facets of society are you called to influence? God wants to expand your vision and the possibilities of how He has uniquely designed and created you to be used! God knows where your anointing, skills and ministry will excel. We are commissioned to bring His kingdom - which is righteousness, peace and joy, wherever we go!

I refuse to lose hope in America! We have so much work ahead of us and this is no time to retreat. We must advance and usher our Nation back to God Almighty! I believe in His everlasting mercies and loving kindness. I believe that He will forgive our transgressions and sins when we repent and return to Him with our whole heart! I believe He will heal our land! I believe we will prevail over the hordes of darkness. Reformation will surely come to our Nation! We are a reformation generation!

Where are we going? Wherever His Spirit beckons! Boldly! We have mountains to capture and nations to disciple! That a generation may see, *"...The kingdoms of this world have become the kingdoms of our Lord and of His Christ, and He shall reign forever and ever!"* (Revelation 11:15)

Isaiah 9:7 | NKJV
"Of the increase of His government and peace There will be no end, Upon the throne of David and over His kingdom, To order it and establish it with judgment and justice From that time forward, even forever. The zeal of the Lord of hosts will perform this."

CHAPTER NINE

THE ULTIMATE COMEBACK

America's Return to The Covenant Keeping God!

W ho doesn't love a comeback? We all love to enjoy movies and story lines that bring triumph from tragedy and victorious hope from hopelessness, because deep inside we know that God wants us to win! Cinderella Man, with Russell Crowe, is among one of our favorites. How about The Count Of Monte Cristo, The Natural or The Dark Knight Rises? How about Elvis' 1968 black leather comeback? Hmmm....that was just for laughs!

I love to watch boxing and football. There's nothing like watching a team rise from the ashes to win in a desperate comeback scenario. Joe Montana became synonymous with "comeback" during his Hall of Fame career. Perhaps none of his heroics were greater than the day in which he led the San Francisco 49ers back from a 28 point deficit. Three amazing plays including a 1-yard run, connecting on a 71-yard bomb and adding another TD pass rallied the 49ers to an incredible win over New Orleans! I'm always on the edge of my seat in any given boxing match, as the exhausted fighter who's been crushed and beaten down, somehow finds the inner strength and momentum to rally back and take the fight!

The Scriptures and history are filled with stories of setbacks and comebacks. Just ask Job, Joseph, Moses, Caleb, Ruth, Naomi, Elijah or Esther about comebacks. How about David, Sampson, Lazarus, Peter, Paul, John Mark, George Washington and Abraham Lincoln, just to name a few. Towering above them all is the greatest ultimate comeback, which stands as the foundation upon which our faith rests secured – Jesus' resurrection! Jesus is the King of the comebacks! His matchless story heralds complete triumph over death, hell and the grave! A lot can change in just 3 days! Lest we forget, He's also due for yet another comeback!

What does an ultimate comeback look like? One of the most beautiful and profound pictures of comeback in the 20th century is that of the Jews (The children of Israel) after World War II. Literally rising out of the ashes of death and the horror of the holocaust, they rose to become a nation once again in May 1948, fulfilling Isaiah's prophesy! *"Who has heard such a thing? Who has seen such things? Shall the earth be made to give birth in one day? Or shall a nation be born at once? For as soon as Zion was in labor, She gave birth to her children."* (Isaiah 66:8)

President Abraham Lincoln's epic comeback story, through setbacks and adversity, is absolutely remarkable! At the tender age of 7, because his family had been forced out of their home, Abe needed to go to work to help support his family. His mother passed away when he was only 9. At 19, his sister died. At age, 22 his business venture failed. He ran for the State Legislature at 23 and lost. In the same year, he also lost his job and decided he wanted to go to law school but couldn't get in. He borrowed money from a friend to start a business and by the end of that year he was bankrupt.

In 1834, at age 25, he ran for the State Legislature again, and this time he won. The following year, things were looking up, as he was engaged to be married. Sadly, his fiancée died and he was grief stricken. He experienced a total nervous breakdown and for 6 months was bedridden! He was only 27 at the time!

In 1836, he contended to become Speaker of the State Legislature but was defeated. In 1840, he sought to become Elector and was defeated. In 1842 he married Mary Todd, and over the years the Lincolns would have 4 boys. Only one would ultimately live to maturity.

In 1843, he ran for Congress and lost, but in 1846 he ran for Congress again and won. He then moved to Washington, DC at the age of 37. In 1848, he ran for re-election to Congress and lost. In 1849, he sought the job as a Land Officer in his home state but failed to get the job. In 1850, his son Edward, died. In 1854, Lincoln ran for the Senate of the United States and lost. In 1856, he sought the Vice Presidential nomination at a national convention and he received humiliation with less than 100 votes! In 1858, he ran for the Senate again…you guessed it…he lost yet again! Lincoln had two business ventures that failed, and lost 8 different elections, as well as having a complete nervous breakdown, all before becoming President of the United States in 1860!

One of my mentors used to say to me – "Your losses aren't your bosses!" That is so true! After overcoming such notable loses, setbacks and even the agony of death, Abraham Lincoln was elected President of the United States in 1860 becoming one of our greatest leaders, a true hero and the great emancipator! Ultimate comebacks are not pretty story lines whatsoever, but they come to those who endure, persevere and never give up! America owes a debt of gratitude to this man who refused to quit, even in his most bleak and challenging times of peril!

Everyone experiences setbacks. You cannot avoid them, no matter who you are and no matter what you do…no one is exempt. Yet, comebacks are possible. A comeback takes uncommon focus, endurance and hard work. Everyone, from ordinary people just like you and me, to Biblical heroes, to professional athletes, have all proven it is possible. And what's more important, with God giving you favor, you can expect an ultimate comeback!

Some of you are presently living the ultimate comeback. You

211

experienced a divorce, a health crisis, you lost a loved one, you suffered major financial loss, you lost your home or your job... whatever the case. Yet, the Lord's faithfulness turned your setback into a testimony of comeback!

Perhaps you are presently facing the greatest setback of your life right now. God's love and grace will empower you to release your regrets...*forgetting those things that are behind you and pressing forward* to make the difficult but necessary adjustments. (Phil 3:12) He will restore your confidence and you will regain momentum in His breath, and dream again. In Zephaniah 3:17 it says, *"The Lord your God wins victory after victory and is always with you."* One thing I know for sure, God wants you to have a comeback, based on the reality of who He is in you!

We all must remember that setbacks do not need to control or define our lives – we control our lives and Christ defines our lives. No matter what has happened, don't allow your setbacks to define you anymore. Become determined to move forward into the dream God has for you. Ask yourself what it is you want more than anything. Then ask yourself how you're going to make it happen. To make the dream a reality, it will require the discipline that matches the desire.

America At The Crossroads
Crossroads: A crisis situation or point in time when a critical decision must be made.

We stand at an absolute pivotal crossroads in our nation's history! I wonder if our founding fathers would even recognize the America that we have become. Our fathers understood that America was God's idea and God's dream. They were determined to build a nation on the true Cornerstone and place our security under His authority and purposes. They feared the Lord and honored His Word. I believe that it is not too late for our prodigal Nation to experience an ultimate comeback. But let's be honest, the real setbacks that we face are the result of our sin, rebellion and rejection of God. Our pride and unrighteous has grieved His heart. The scriptures teach that *"righteousness exalts a nation and the nation is blessed whose God is the Lord"* (Proverbs 14:34 & Psalm 33:12).

Abraham Lincoln understood this and wrote it in his proclamation: *"We have been the recipients of the choicest bounties of heaven. We have been preserved, these many years, in peace and prosperity. We have grown in numbers, wealth and power, as no other nation has ever grown. But we have forgotten God...We have forgotten the gracious hand which preserved us in peace, and multiplied and enriched and strengthened us... and we have vainly imagined, in the deceitfulness of our hearts, that all these blessings were produced by some superior wisdom and virtue of our own...Intoxicated with unbroken success, we have become too self-sufficient to feel the necessity of redeeming and preserving grace, too proud to pray to the God that made us! It behooves us, then to humble ourselves before the offended Power, to confess our national sins, and* to pray for clemency and forgiveness." (Proclamation for a National Day of Fasting, Humiliation & Prayer, April 30, 1863)

These penetrating words hit the bulls-eye again, over 150 years later! We have lost our way, friends! But we can find our way back - and we must. The only way to recapture our Nation is to return to the covenant keeping God.

Covenant

Over 4,000 years ago, The Lord appeared to Abraham and made a covenant with him, *"...through you all the nations of the earth all be blessed"* which became an irrevocable link - heaven to earth - to bestow blessing and power upon all mankind. (Genesis 22) The founding fathers of America understood the power of God's everlasting covenant and sought to establish our Nation based upon the honor of His Word.

God is the covenant-keeping God. God kept His covenant with Abraham, Isaac, and Jacob. The "covenant family" eventually went down into Egypt and multiplied greatly, but came under miserable slavery. What is it that sets up the story of the exodus and conquest of the Promised Land? We read in Exodus 2:24, *"And God heard their groaning, and God remembered His covenant with Abraham, with Isaac, and with Jacob."* The background for the redemption from Egypt, and the rest of the Biblical story, is precisely the covenant-keeping character of God. He is the God of the covenant. What God revealed through Moses was the law, but specifically the law "of the *covenant"* (Ex. 34:27-28). And as Israel prepared to enter the promised land, Moses reminded God's people of the basis and character of their blessing: *"Therefore know that the Lord your God, He is God, the faithful God who keeps covenant and mercy for a thousand generations with those who love Him and keep His commandments..."*(Deut. 7:9).

God made a "covenant" with David and his seed (2 Sam. 23:5; Ps. 89). Many years later, in the days of Isaiah, God declared *"I will make an everlasting covenant with you, even the sure mercies of David"* (Isaiah 55:3). When Jeremiah the prophet ministered to God's people, God revealed the coming of that day, when all of His previous promises would come to realization and fulfillment - in the days of a "new *covenant"* (Jeremiah 31:31-34).

We cannot comprehend the saving work of our Lord Jesus Christ without a covenantal perspective. The birth of Jesus was an open declaration that God had remembered "his holy *covenant"* (Luke 1:72). Before Jesus was crucified he ordained the cup of the "new *covenant"* (Luke 22:20). His resurrection and redemptive work were specifically the blessing of *"the covenant God made with your fathers"* (Acts 3:25-26). The New Testament explicitly calls Jesus *"the Mediator of the New Covenant"* (Heb. 12:24) and views His work of salvation in covenantal terms: *"Now the God of peace who brought again from the dead our Lord Jesus, that great shepherd of* the sheep, *through the blood of the everlasting covenant..."* (Heb. 13:20).

God has provided every person with the ability to experience the ultimate comeback by His very own Son. The blood of His New Covenant is the testament of eternal love and redemption. A covenant is something that God makes with man. It is the Sovereign dispensing of His grace, and the security attached to the covenant arises or rests in the action of God. It is God who makes the covenant, and it is God who ensures that it continues, remains in force or ceases to be. This action is not ours. However, it is true that there are obligations in the covenant, and that these obligations are constructed by God.

Without question, the cornerstone of each covenant is that God will keep His promise. The question has never been, can we trust God? The question is, can God trust us to hold to our obligation of covenant keeping?

The Burning Lamp

Genesis 15:17 | ESV
"When the sun had gone down and it was dark, behold a smoking fire pot and a flaming torch passed between these pieces."

In this profound revelation of covenant, God reveals His honor and integrity by the fire of His Presence. In Abraham's day, when covenants were made, certain rites would accompany the agreement, in order to signify what would happen if one or both parties failed to live up to their end of the pact. One common ritual involved dismembering animals and then laying the pieces in two rows side-by-side, with a path laid in between. The individuals making the covenant would then pass between the animals and invoke a curse upon themselves if they broke the agreement. In performing this rite, both parties were in effect saying, "If I do not fulfill the terms of this covenant, may the destruction that came upon these animals also be upon my head."

Amazingly, as if His word of promise were not enough, The Lord finishes His encounter with Abram in Genesis 15 with this very same rite. This theophany (a visible revelation of the Divine) is in God's appearance as a smoking fire pot and a flaming torch, just as He appeared to Moses and Israel as a pillar of fire, guiding toward Canaan centuries later. (Exodus 13:21-22) Fire symbolizes the Lord's glory, holiness and character.

The Scriptures reveal that God alone is the Burning One, who passes between the animals; Abram is not invited to participate.

Here we have the Lord alone swearing by Himself that He will see to it that His promises for an everlasting covenant for all generations will come to pass! This sworn oath is promissory (invoking death to Himself if it is not fulfilled), giving His people confidence that He is trustworthy to accomplish all that He pledges. It is an unprecedented manifestation of the Lord's grace, as He promises to care for Abraham, His loyal friend, and his descendents forever!

Hebrews 6:13-18 | NKJV
"For when God made a promise to Abraham, because He could swear by no one greater, He swore by Himself, saying, "Surely blessing I will bless you, and multiplying I will multiply you." And so, after he had patiently endured, he obtained the promise. For men indeed swear by the greater, and an oath for confirmation is for them an end of all dispute. Thus God, determining to show more abundantly to the heirs of promise the immutability of His counsel, confirmed it by an oath, that by two immutable things, in which it is impossible for God to lie, we might have strong consolation, who have fled for refuge to lay hold of the hope set before us."

It is important to recognize that this profound grace does not abolish Abram's responsibility to continue his loyalty and obligation to follow God faithfully. However, God knowing all things, recognized that though His people may at times be disloyal, He structured the covenant to fully keep His end of the bargain! This is Love!

The Father's promise to Abraham, unfolding throughout the generations, found its' consummation in the revealing of His Beloved Son, thus securing all of the blessings He promised that day, through His own death. When God made his covenant to Abraham, He knew that He would be the one to bear our curse and judgment!

Galatians 3:13 | MSG
"Christ redeemed us from that self-defeating, cursed life by absorbing it completely into himself. Do you remember the Scripture that says, "Cursed is everyone who hangs on a tree"? That is what happened when Jesus was nailed to the cross: He became a curse, and at the same time

dissolved the curse. And now, because of that, the air is cleared and we can see that Abraham's blessing is present and available for non-Jews, too. We are all able to receive God's life, his Spirit, in and with us by believing — just the way Abraham received it."

2 Corinthians 5:21 | NKJV
"For He made Him who knew no sin to be sin for us, that we might become the righteousness of God in Him."

This is Love! When the Burning One gives His Word, He keeps His Word. Stop for a moment and just consider how amazing it is that God, who will not suffer any loss of His glory, would put His honor at stake, in His plan to bring redemption to the world. He *is* the covenant keeping God!

2 Chronicles 6:14 | NKJV
"Lord God of Israel, there is no God in heaven or on earth like You, who keep Your covenant and mercy with Your servants who walk before You with all their hearts."

Our prodigal Nation's only hope is the covenant keeping God. The God of Abraham, Isaac and Jacob is JESUS – The Burning Man! He is the unstoppable and unquenchable fire! Just as God heralded through the prophet, Jeremiah, His marriage covenant - forever loyal & faithful - to a backsliding Israel, so The Lord cries out to America! Oh, return America! Return from your backsliding and iniquity! Hear His merciful call. He does not delight in judgment... His mercy triumphs over judgment. We must, like our founding fathers before us, acknowledge and repent of our transgressions... put away our abominations against The Lord God, that He may cleanse us and heal our land.

God longs to avert judgment!

"...Return to Me; And if you will put away your abominations out of My sight, Then you shall not be moved. And you shall swear, 'The Lord lives,' In truth, in judgment, and in righteousness; The nations shall bless themselves in Him, And in Him they shall glory."
Jeremiah 4:1&2 | NKJV

One Nation Under God

The day was April 30th 1789. This was a day of making covenant with God for America. A proclamation was made for the sacred gathering at Federal Hall. "Come and see your President take his oath and pray that God will accept this land as His". At 9am the bells pealed throughout the city. George Washington made his oath of office in New York City. He laid his hand on the Bible, (and not merely on the Bible. He opened it up and laid his hand upon and the covenant God had made with Abraham). Then lifting his other arm upward toward to heaven, Washington made a vow to lead our nation and honor the God of Israel and His covenant. (I think it's notable that the only other President to do this was Ronald Reagan.) After Washington invoked his oath and covenant unto the Lord and sealed it with – "so help me God", he bowed his knee to the ground in reverence and kissed the Bible. Afterward, Washington called the senators, and newly elected officials to join him, as they walked arm in arm down the streets of New York to St. Paul's Chapel. There they bowed together, prayed and dedicated this land – America - to God! The day that George Washington was inaugurated was the day that covenant was invoked. America belonged to God Almighty!

I stand first and foremost as a Christian and with millions of courageous patriots as a witness with George Washington, Thomas Jefferson, James Madison, John Adams, and countless other American patriots from our beginnings until this day, to testify that *America is One Nation Under God!* Though we have strayed from His grace, we must remember our covenant and vow to the Lord!

On May 17, 1776, our Congress prayed for divine favor. They declared a "Day of Humiliation, Fasting and Prayer" throughout the colonies. The day was set apart and called sacred unto the Lord to *". . . confess and bewail our manifold sins and transgressions, and by a sincere repentance and amendment of life, appease his displeasure, and through the merits and mediation of Jesus Christ, obtain his pardon and forgiveness."* They didn't call out to Allah (the moon god), Buddha, or to one of the 330 million false gods of Hinduism...they called upon the Name that is above every name – that of The King of

Kings and Lord of Lords!

Psalm 33:12 | NKJV
"Blessed is the nation whose God is the Lord..."

Friends, when we take God out of America, we lose! When we honor Him as our Lord and God, we win! We presently have a culture and government that embraces and openly celebrates all that God says is wrong. Many Christians are ready to throw up their hands and say we have no power to change America and all is lost. But that is not true! All is not lost! Make no mistake; today plays a very important role in American history and we must pray and repent. We must return to the covenant keeping One – The Lord Jesus Christ! Never underestimate the prayers of the righteous! God hears those who are His! He knows His covenant keepers. His remnant will raise the banner high and call America back to His throne of grace!

Will We Humble Ourselves & Repent?

2 Chronicles 7:14 | NKJV
"... if My people who are called by My name will humble themselves, and pray and seek My face, and turn from their wicked ways, then I will hear from heaven, and will forgive their sin and heal their land."

America's ultimate comeback rests upon this command – will we repent and turn from our sin and wickedness? Will we truly humble ourselves before the Lord and confess that we have betrayed Him? Will we turn from our corruption, iniquities and transgressions? Will we open our hard and impenitent hearts to repent of our unfaithfulness? Will we awaken to His love and mercy? Do we really understand that without Him, all will be lost? We must believe and contend for awakening and reformation in our generation! His blood and grace is still amazing to forgive, heal and deliver us from evil!

God's will and God's obligation are two different things entirely. Without a doubt, it is God's will to heal and restore America, but if we do not fully repent and come to Him, He is fully obligated to deal with us according to His Word. Every parent understands this.

My heart aches for America. These days are very dark, but there is still hope! My fervent prayer is that we are on the edge of a new Great Awakening right now! It has been said that its *always darkest before the dawn,* and that has always been true in America, before every great spiritual movement. This was true before the First Great Awakening, the Second Great Awakening and all other awakenings. In that darkness, God's people united in prayer to turn the tide!

Nineveh was the lone world superpower – wealthy, unconcerned and self-centered - filled with wickedness in Jonah's time. When the prophet finally abandoned his deliberate disobedience and surrendered to the Word of the Lord, proclaiming God's warning to Nineveh, the people heard, awakened and repented! I believe the same thing can happen once again, this time in our nation. Our Lord is a God of mercy and longsuffering. He is slow to anger and great in kindness. He has promised to always respond to a repentant heart. If we do not repent, America will undoubtedly face the fiery judgment of God.

The blood of the new covenant that Jesus shed on a cross, on a hill in Jerusalem, cries out mercy to us! When America turns to the crucified and resurrected One, then we will behold The Burning Lamp, The Unstoppable and Unquenchable One. Then we will witness Him from coast to coast, from sea to shining sea, as He reaches down to cleanse and heal us by His own Blood, pouring His everlasting mercies upon America!

God Loves America! He has not abandoned us, and His love for our Nation has not diminished or withered. His hope is alive, burning and pulsating with everlasting Love. He is the Everlasting and Ever Faithful One. He is the Covenant keeping God! America is a special treasure to The Lord. She has been a catalyst to spread the knowledge of the Gospel of Jesus Christ to the earth, and now she must once again awaken to the voice of God!

Jesus is the hope of the nations, and He is the only true source for our ultimate comeback!

CHAPTER TEN

LET HOPE ARISE

"Now may the God of hope fill you with all joy and peace in believing, that you may abound in hope by the power of the Holy Spirit."
Romans 15:13

On October 4th, 1997, more than 1.4 million Christian men gathered on the Mall in Washington D.C. for what was described by Promise Keepers as a "sacred assembly". Men traveled across the country to spend 1 day together in prayerful repentance for their individual sins and the sins of our Nation. The bus trip to D.C. was a sobering ten hours for me. As I prayed quietly beneath my breath, I began to sense the magnitude of this historic gathering. God was lifting my hope and my vision higher for America, and I was embracing my call as a watchman and intercessor.

The sight of more than 1 million men bowing before the Lord was remarkable. The Mall became a threshing floor for God to come and extend His mercy and loving kindness. I knelt in the grass and laid face down before the Lord. I was enveloped with sorrow, pain and deep grief. The gravity and magnitude of our country's rebellion against God was overwhelming to me. The Holy Spirit was letting me feel just a touch of how we have broken the Father's heart and His deep longings for the prodigal nation to return home.

The sound of multitudes of grown men weeping and crying out for forgiveness was beyond anything I can effectively convey to you... and has never left me. There's a song from the early 90's that I have loved for many years by Bob Carlisle that says, *"When a grown man cries, you can feel the thunder, he can call down angels with sign and wonders. He's a powerful man with a weary soul and his tears can touch the very heart of God...when a grown man cries."* The Scripture says that when we sow with tears, we will reap with joy! (Psalm 126:5) This trip profoundly energized my hope and watered my seeds of consecration to *stand in the gap* – to never relent in intercession for revival and for our Nation's ultimate comeback.

The "sacred assembly" in Washington became a catalyst that gave birth to many national ministries and movements that have been rallying this generation to seek the face of God! One of the pioneers whom God raised up was Lou Engle, a prophet and intercessor. He rallied hundreds of thousands of passionate young people with "The Call". For the last 17 years, The Call has been invading college campuses and stadiums from coast to coast to pray and fast for the reformation of our Nation!

As I fast forward in time and look across the present natural and spiritual landscape of 2014, regardless of our present circumstances, I am anchored in my hope, anticipating the greatest revival and reformation we have ever known. For the last several decades, the Holy Spirit has ignited prayer movements throughout America, awakening the church from its slumber. God's people are praying and taking courageous action! The battle for the soul of our nation has been epic, but I believe our greatest hour is not behind us but still ahead!

Is there hope for America? Yes! Abounding hope! I believe the move of God that America is going to experience will be so transforming that it is beyond anything we have ever conceptually imagined! Our hope must be anchored in who is forever constant – our God! Circumstances and seasons change; but Jesus is the same yesterday, today and forever!

"Now faith is the substance (assurance) of things hoped for, the evidence (conviction) of things not seen."
Hebrews 11:1 | NKJV

Biblical hope is not wishful thinking. Real biblical hope is anchored in the Word of God as its foundation. Hope is the joyful and confident expectation of the goodness of God. The root of all genuine, authentic, mountain-moving faith is knowing that God's heart and intentions toward us are good and blessed! Remember that God told Jeremiah that His plans are to give us hope (an expected end) and a brighter future! (Jeremiah 29:11) True biblical hope is certainty not probability. God is worthy of our absolute assurance. He will never fail us. Hope flows from the covenant relationship we have with Christ who is the centerpiece and cornerstone of our hope. He is Living Hope!

"In his name the nations will put their hope."
Matthew 12:21 | NIV

America needs messengers of hope right now! In this present hour, it is critically important that we learn to live out of a reservoir and stronghold of hope, and become conduits of His life and releasers of that hope. Have you noticed that the enemy hates hope and confidence? Because it's powerful! That's why he is constantly bombarding believers with discouragement. Many today are living in survival mode, simply espousing "make it through mindsets". But hope is an "expansion" mindset! The kingdom of God is about an ever increasing and expanding hope mindset. God has not forsaken us and we are not destined to just survive in an hour of crisis. In Psalm 71, David proclaims that God has been and forever will be his stronghold of hope. David says, *"As for me, I will hope continuously; I will praise you more and more."* I've made the decision that as for me and my house, we are going to hope in the Lord our God! The essence of hope is a place of peace and rest. God is our security and our refuge!

On the steps of the Lincoln Memorial, in August of 1963, Martin Luther King Jr. thundered his famous and dynamic "I Have A Dream" speech to more than 250,000 civil rights supporters. One of the prophetic lines from that speech, which is inscribed on the cornerstone of his memorial in Washington is: *"With this faith we will be able to hew out of a mountain of despair, a stone of hope"*. I want to hew out a legacy of hope for our children and our children's children...for generations that are yet to come! I'm declaring that these present mountains of despair can melt like wax in the Presence of the Lord!

No Cost Is Too Great

Hope reformers are coming to restore our foundations. True reformation and true revival is not neat and sanitary...it's going to get messy...but its necessary! People often romanticize visions of change, but the truth is, the cost of reformation is extreme. It will cost you everything...including your reputation. If you are going to speak truth in this hostile culture you will undoubtedly be mocked and persecuted. William Booth, the founder of The Salvation Army said, *"It seems that God cannot do anything on the planet earth unless a few good men are willing to go to jail."* It's no coincidence that most of the New Testament was written from a jail cell. Paul was a reformer. Most of the prophets were in jail. Why? Because preaching the kingdom of God brings one into conflict with earthly tyranny. Make no mistake, it is going to require tremendous courage in this hour! The mark of a true servant of God is his or her willingness to suffer shame and rejection for the Master!

The high price for standing for the truth will never be marked down or go on sale. The prophet Isaiah was put into a hollow log and sawed in half. Jeremiah endured opposition, beatings and imprisonment - was abducted and taken to Egypt. Daniel was thrown into a lion's den. Hananiah, Mishael and Azariah were thrown into the fiery furnace because they refused to bow and worship a Babylonian false god. John the Baptist had his head cut off and served on a platter for a party display. Jesus was a man of many sorrows and well acquainted with grief. He was lifted up upon a cross and crucified in the prime of his life. Eleven of the twelve disciples died a martyr's death. Andrew and Bartholomew were crucified. James, the son of Alphaeus, was stoned to death. James, the son of Zebedee was beheaded. His brother John was boiled in oil and banished to the island of Patmos. Peter and Philip were crucified upside down. Thomas was martyred in India. The Apostle Paul was stoned, beaten and finally beheaded. Church history is bloody with the sacrifice of suffering and conviction. William Tyndale was hung. His then dead body was burned at a stake, for translating the Bible into the English language for common people to read. John Hus was burned at the stake. Martin Luther had a bounty on his head. The blood of the Scottish Covenanters flowed down the streets of Edinburgh. I could go on and on...Jonathan Edwards, the leader of the Great Awakening, was expelled from his pulpit and pastorate after 23 years of faithful ministry by a 90% vote. George Whitfield, the great evangelist, was shut out of all the pulpits of England and was forced to go into the open fields to preach.

In First Corinthians, Paul pours out his heart. Here, he shares how the true apostles and reformers were received by the world and the church – derided and reviled as scum. *"For I think that God has displayed us, the apostles, last, as men condemned to death; for we have been made a spectacle to the world, both to angels and to men. We are fools for Christ's sake, but you are wise in Christ! We are weak, but you are strong! You are distinguished, but we are dishonored! To the present hour we both hunger and thirst, and we are poorly clothed, and beaten, and homeless. And we labor, working with our own hands. Being reviled, we bless; being persecuted, we endure; being defamed, we entreat. We have been made as the scum of the earth, the offscouring of all things until now.* (1 Corinthians 4:9-13) I remember when Bren and I stood quietly and reverently in the Coliseum of Rome, honoring the memory of those Christians who had been condemned to death, paying the ultimate sacrifice for their faith in Jesus! Here's the point – all who share in Christ's riches will also share in His suffering. (Philippians 3:10) The awakening that is just beginning to break forth in this hour will surely "separate the men from the boys" so to speak. Many believers in our generation are going to have to come to grips with a certain reality. Do they possess mere preferences or deep abiding convictions? Let me tell it to you straight – it will cost you everything to courageously follow Jesus! There will be great opposition, challenges, difficulty, trials and suffering in the days and years ahead. But there is no price too great! He is our Reward!

"Blessed are those who are persecuted for righteousness' sake, for theirs is the kingdom of heaven. "Blessed are you when they revile and persecute you, and say all kinds of evil against you falsely for My sake. Rejoice and be exceedingly glad, for great is your reward in heaven, for so they persecuted the prophets who were before you."
Matthew 5:10-12 | NKJV

*"Therefore, having been justified by faith, we have peace with God through our Lord Jesus Christ, through whom also we have access by faith into this grace in which we stand, and **rejoice in hope of the glory of God. And not only that, but we also glory in tribulations, knowing that tribulation produces perseverance; and perseverance, character; and character, hope. Now hope does not lead to disappointment, because the love of God has been poured out in our hearts by the Holy Spirit who was given to us."***
Romans 5:1-5 | NKJV

In the midst of pressure and these trying times, I am confident that God sees what we cannot. He is at work building us for a victory that will be unprecedented. We will overcome, and we will persevere. Perseverance is having the capacity to bear up under difficult obstacles and circumstances. Perseverance is not just the ability to simply survive. No, it's far greater than that. By persevering, one becomes a person who is able to bear spiritual weight! God is working and making you into a man or woman who is absolutely amazing – tested and true – embodying truth, wisdom and gold, tried in the fire! You would never have been able to bear up under such weightiness, unless you would have persevered in tribulation. Through perseverance, proven character is that which has been tested, and found to be pure and authentic. Character gives birth to hope which empowers us to overcome! Do not underestimate the value of your process of development. Hope reformers are born in the fire! Hope reformers are anchored in Christ and prepared for the day of victory!

We must not grow weary while doing good, for in due season we shall reap if we do not lose heart. (Galatians 6:9) This is no time to lose heart... *"Therefore, strengthen your feeble arms and weak knees."* (Hebrews 12:12) We must pray continuously and advance courageously prevailing over the darkness!

God's hope reformers will shift the atmospheres of cities and regions! You must refuse to allow discouragement and fear to mislead you concerning America's future. Biblical hope is based on the covenant we have with God. Hope comes when we receive the promises of God and begin to see ourselves with what God has promised us - instead of seeing ourselves without it. When you have hope, you have a supernatural expectation that what God has said will certainly come to pass in your life. It would be easy in the natural to give into despair and hopelessness, but I refuse! More than ever, we must hold fast to our confession of hope!

Hebrews 10:23 | NKJV
"Let us hold fast the confession of our hope without wavering, for He who promised is faithful."

Our God is faithful! Perhaps He has saved his best and finest wine for such a time as this! In an atmosphere and climate that looked absolutely hopeless, Abraham chose to have hope! Romans 4:18 & 20 *"... who, contrary to hope, in hope believed, so that he became the father of many nations, according to what was spoken, 'So shall your descendants be...' He did not waver at the promise of God through unbelief, but was strengthened in faith, giving glory to God, and being fully convinced that what He had promised He was also able to perform."* More than ever, we cannot waver and fall into unbelief that our Nation will not return to God. Let hope arise!

Hebrews 6:9 | NKJV
"This hope is a strong and trustworthy anchor for our souls..."

Hope is an anchor in the abiding presence of God. A life must be properly anchored, because if it's not, it has the potential to drift. You can drift so far that you may wind up somewhere you were never supposed to be. It is no secret that our Nation has drifted far away from godly fear and honor of The King. When people lose hope it affects their imagination. Hopelessness is being convinced there isn't anything beyond what has already been seen. That's why people are killing each other in our streets, sticking needles in their arms, putting drugs up their nose, committing suicide, young women aborting and terminating their future...why? No hope!

When I was a boy growing up on the Illinois River, I used to have an old dog named, Snoopy. From time to time Snoopy would disappear for the day. He would take off exploring. He had a crazy obsession. He would roll around in dead fish. When he'd come home, reeking of dead carp and fish innards, my Dad would make me chain him up and wash him down. Oh my...I hated washing that dog! That's what people do when they have no hope, they go running to roll around in the filth of sin and enjoy drifting with the stench of death on them. Why? They've lost their anchor. They've lost their hope. Jesus is the only strong and trustworthy anchor for one's life, and for that of our Nation - clearly adrift! Furthermore, He is the only one who can wash our sins away!

Proverbs, 13:12 says, *"Hope deferred makes the heart sick, but a dream fulfilled is a tree of life."* The delay of earnest desires and expectation can become like an affliction. But the scripture doesn't stop there...*"a dream fulfilled is like a tree of life."* – When the hope and dreams of desires are obtained it becomes *a tree of life.* The picture of eating from the tree of life is one of refreshing fulfillment. It's reviving to the soul. Far too many people have pitched their tent in the lands of no hope. I've been told many times by well meaning people, *"Don't get your hopes up."* Has that ever happened to you? Perhaps that's what you've told yourself. That's poor advice. Faith has no action whatsoever if hope is not alive. We must not only get our hopes up, but we must let our hope free to fly and soar, high above the present circumstances, and see a new vantage point – a heavenly perspective.

When my hope is flying and soaring high above like a mighty eagle, I can see the storm of fire upon the horizon coming to America! The unstoppable and unquenchable One has set His blazing affection upon us! A *"storm"* can be defined as a *disturbance in the air above the earth in the atmosphere, manifesting itself by winds of unusual force or direction, often accompanied by rain, snow, hail, thunder, and lightning, or flying sand or dust or a heavy fall of rain, snow, or hail, or a violent outbreak of thunder and lightning, unaccompanied by strong winds. In the verb tense it means to attack, to rush upon or capture a place, to deliver a violent attack or fire, as with artillery.*

"Then I looked, and behold, a whirlwind was coming out of the north, a great cloud with raging fire engulfing itself; and bright-ness was all around it and radiating out of its midst like the color of amber, out of the midst of the fire."
Ezekiel 1:4 | NKJV

The glory of the Lord is going to storm upon our Nation with holy fire – with thunderings, lightings and power! The clouds of hope are billowing even now to counter and crush the demonic storms and activity hovering over our Nation. A heavenly intervention is upon us to meet the crisis of this hour. This coming move of The Spirit will be radical, with signs, wonders and unprecedented harvest! These are the days of living revelation, living hope and divine alignment with the Spirit of God. A third great awakening and reformation is dawning!

The Burning One who makes the clouds His chariot and walks upon the wind, is coming to set the church on fire and our Nation ablaze! (Psalm 104:3) May your heart encounter the Holy Spirit afresh! May you receive the baptism of fire and love! May you become an unstoppable agent of change, invading the darkness and transforming lives! My prayer for you is that He will envelop and encompass you in His all-consuming love - that you will become a catalyst, revealing His burning heart to this generation and those that are yet to come!

Arise and burn! Christ in you is the unstoppable and unquench-able fire! The best is yet to come! Forward!

ENDNOTES

1. Page 27 http://frankbartleman-azusa.blogspot.com/2008/10/pastor-smale-returns-from-wales.html

2. Page 29 http://www.revival-library.org/pensketches/am_pentecostals/seymourazusa.html

3. Page 44 John G. Lake, Spiritual Hunger & other Sermons by Gordon Lindsay (Christ For The Nations 1987 pages 7,13&14) http://www.fire-school.org/media/articles/fall-on-your-face-and-pray/ & http://www.voiceofrevolution.com/2012/07/05/fall-on-your-face-and-pray-dr-michael-brown/

4. Page 103 Meth In America. http://www.policymic.com/articles/65703/how-much-meth-does-your-state-cook-these-maps-show-the-drug-s-foothold-in-america

5. Page 109 Charles Finney, Lectures on Revivals of Religion (Oberlin, Ohio: EJ Goodrich, 1868 page 15)

6. Page 111 Booth, General "Who Cares?" 1912 The Authoritative Life of General William Booth: Founder of the Salvation Army By George Scott Railton. General Booth: His passion for the lost, especially those who were considered "irredeemable" by the established church, was legendary. His whole life can be summed up in his own words, "Go for souls - and go for the worst!"

7. Page 114 John Wesley & Cane Ridge (Historical Collections of Ohio & Encyclopedia of The State Volume 2 page 461 Henry Howe & A Cure For All Ills 1988, page33&34) & (Christian History, 1995, Issue 45, Revival At Cain Ridge) Cane Ridge quotes: The Cure of All Ills, Mary Stuart Relfe pg.49 & Historical Collections of Ohio and Encyclopedia of The State Volume 2. Pg 461

8. Page 115 Jeremiah Lanphier & 1857 Revival (Mary Stuart Relfe, Cure of all Ills, page 49) Prayer Gatherings (THE LAYMAN'S PRAYER REVIVAL 1857-58 By Oliver Price)

9. Page 116 1857 Revival (From J. Edwin Orr, The Light of the Nations pp. 103-105)

10. Page 116 & 117 Alex de Tocqueville, thought not a quote from his books, this statement is routinely and widely accepted as one made by Tocqueville

11. Page 118 Azusa, David Garcia (From "They Told Me Their Stories", Tommy Welchel pg. 100-101)

12. Page 119 (Camp Meeting, July 1994, Louisville KY with Rodney Howard-Browne)

13. Page 120 Quote on Charles Finney. (Perry Miller, Book: Charles Finney, cover)

14. Page 131 Washington Footnotes: Description by Washington Irving, as quoted in Bennet, 368 http://www.archives.gov/legislative/features/gw-inauguration/ From Marshall and Manuel, 357 . 1776 http://www.loc.gov/exhibits/religion/rel04.html

15. Page 194 http://www.forerunner.com/forerunner/X0587_Charles_G._Finney.html

16. Page 195 http://www.goodreads.com/quotes/1008646-i-sought-for-the-greatness-and-genius-of-america-in

17. Page 197 http://www.dealpentecostal.co.uk/They%20told%20me%20their%20stories%20ebook.pdf (page 38)

Recommended Reading For
The Burning Hearts

The Revival Study Bible
William Seymour | **The Great Azusa Street Revival**
Rick Joyner | **The World On Fire**
Bill Johnson | **When Heaven Invades Earth**
Tommy Welchel | **Azusa Street: They Told Me Their Stories**
Rick Joyner | **The Power To Change The World**
Tommy Tenney | **The God Chasers**
AW Tozer | **Knowledge of The Holy**
AW Tozer | **The Pursuit of His Presence**
Tommy Tenney | **God's Favorite House**
Dutch Sheets | **The Pioneer Spirit**
Leif Hetland | **Seeing Through Heavens Eyes**
Steve Hill | **A Time To Weep**
Mary Stewart Relfe | **The Cure For All Ills**
Dutch Sheets | **Intercessory Prayer**
Aimee Simple McPherson | **This Is That**
Randy Clark | **There Is More**
Bill Johnson | **Hosting The Presence**
John G. Lake | **Diary of God's Generals**
Jack Hayford | **The Charismatic Century**
(The Enduring Impact of the Azusa Street Revival)
Kenneth Copeland | **John G. Lake: His Life, His Sermons, His Boldness of Faith**
Watchman Nee | **The Normal Christian Life**
Bill Johnson | **Experience The Impossible**
Leonard Ravenhill | **Why Revival Tarries**
Roberts Liardon | **God's Generals I, II & III**
Winkie Pratney | **Revival**
Kris Vallotton | **Developing A Supernatural Lifestyle**
Mike Bickle | **Passion For Jesus**
John Sherrill | **They Speak With Other Tongues**
Eddie Hyatt and Joel Kilpatrick | **The Azusa Street Revival**
Danny Silk | **A Culture Of Honor**
Lance Wallnau & Bill Johnson | **Invading Babylon**
Larry Stockstill | **The Remnant**

Eddie Hyatt | **Fire On The Earth**
Bill Johnson | **Dreaming With God**
C. Peter Wagner | **Radical Holiness for Radical Living**
Craig Borlase | **William Seymour (A Biography)**
Maria Woodworth-Etter | **A Diary of Signs & Wonders**
Che' Ahn | **The Reformers Pledge**
Frank DeCenso | **Amazed By the Power Of God**
Smith Wigglesworth | **Greater Works**
John Greenfield | **Power From On High; The Great
Moravian Revival of 1727**

ABOUT BRIAN GIBBS

B R I A N G I B B S is a husband, father, friend, pastor, revivalist, intercessor, writer and catalyst of hope contending for revival and reformation to recapture America and The Nations. Brian is the founder of Light The Fire Ministries. His ministry is marked with diversity of igniting revival, pastoring, church planting, building leaders and rescuing the broken. Many know him as a national and international revivalist. He is a burning messenger for our times.

Those who know Brian personally know his greatest passions in life are his relationship with his Lord, his wife Bren, and their two children. For the last 20+ years, God has used the Gibbs to empower and mobilize the Body of Christ throughout the USA, Canada, Italy, Sweden, Pakistan, India and Central America. Their ministry is one marked with uncommon favor, wonders and the fire of God.

Brian & Bren reside with their two children & little Shih Tzu in Sarasota, FL.

Light The Fire Ministries
IGNITING Revival | EQUIPPING Leaders | RESCUING The Broken

Mailing:
LTFM | Brian & Bren Gibbs
P.O. BOX 51586
Sarasota, FL 34232

For Booking & Resources
www.lightthefireministries.org
brian@lightthefireministries.org

Social Media
facebook.com/light.the.fire.ministries
facebook.com/brian.gibbs.90

Made in the USA
Charleston, SC
06 February 2016